SURVIVE YOUR CHILD'S SUICIDE

HOW TO MOVE THROUGH GRIEF TO HEALING

PEGGY GREEN

Survive Your Child's Suicide:
How to Move through Grief to Healing
Published by Tie-Dye Press
Denver, CO

ISBN: 979-8-9862270-0-9
SELF-HELP / Death, Grief, Bereavement

Cover and interior design by Victoria Wolf, wolfdesignandmarketing. com. Copyright owned by Peggy Green.

CONTENTS

DEDICATION

Children who die by suicide do so because they want to end their pain, not necessarily because they have a death wish. Unknowingly, they leave a wake of grief, pain, and suffering for those who love them. Their one decision to end their life changes the trajectory of those left behind. I am one of those whose life has been altered. However, I am not the only one. You most likely picked up this book, because your child died by suicide, or you know someone who is experiencing the same pain and suffering.

Suicide among children runs rampant. They could be ten years old, fifteen, forty, fifty, or older. No matter their age, they are still your child and hold a special place in your heart. Their mother still loves them.

This book, with its resources and tools is dedicated to mothers who are doing their best to survive their child's suicide. These tools are 100 percent responsible for me being able to not only survive but thrive in the aftermath of my son's death.

This book is also dedicated to your children who have gone before you. They are missed. They are loved. Their memory is still alive.

To my own son, Connor Bray Green, who left this world way too early. I feel your presence and know you are with me.

Connor/Conman/Buddy/Captain Cagniglio, "I love you to the stars and back!"

Madre/Mom/Mother, "Times three!"

ACKNOWLEDGMENTS

Not to be cliché, but God had his hand in writing this book. My words were guided through Him to create this message. While the death of my son is a horrible tragedy, I now help other mothers who have experienced the same loss.

I have worked with multiple coaches through the years. Business and personal development have been my favorite areas. Each coach has given me at least one golden nugget toward being a better person. Marci McGee, Certified Life Coach, for helping with my mindset and catching me when I get off track. Nick and Megan Unsworth, for Life on Fire Academy and letter to myself. Mary Gaul, Success Magnified — Business Coach, who taught me to focus on the important things in life and helped me make finishing this book a priority. Darren Hardy, for *Darren Daily* that starts my mornings off on a positive note. Brendon Burchard, Growth Day — High Performance Coach, for his incredible energy, reminding me to bring my best every day.

Polly L., you have been amazing in getting this book published and in the hands of those who need it most. Patrice R.B., thanks for doing the fine tuning. Judy R., for telling me before my first book was completed that I would write a second, a third, and many more. Luann C., your impeccable proof reading.

To my friends, old and new — B.C. (before Connor died) and A.C. (after Connor died) — in giving me space when needed, tissues to wipe away my tears, and hugs without being asked: Lisa S., Roxane A., Kathy P., Lisa C., Holly F.

To Jo M., my massage therapist who knew exactly how to take away my tension and release the knots in my neck, shoulders, and back.

To my family who has gone before me. My first daughter Courtney, at nine months who taught me life is short, and every moment needs to be cherished. My dad, who taught me how to garden, wire a light, and experience new things. My mom, who taught me empathy and caring. My sister and best friend, Penny, I miss you every day.

To my daughters, Brittany and Hannah. For I know they too are missing their brother. I wish I could take away your pain. Thank you for your contributions to the title and back cover design.

To Thaide, my nephew, who's humor keeps things lighthearted. And to my niece, Mickey, who has been my sounding board.

To the family I gained, Jason, Bregan, grandson Jameson, and granddaughter Eliora. Thank you for your time in the A.C. era.

To the countless others who have touched my life, I say thank you.

While they will never know the support they have given, I am grateful for the unconditional love of my dog, Kahlua, and cat, Pinball.

CHAPTER 1

YOU CAN MOVE
THROUGH GRIEF
AND HEAL

You are reading this book because you lost a child to suicide. A child can be a young person in their teens or well into their adult years. It does not matter their age. Your grief and pain have been consuming you. Now, you want to move through your loss and reclaim hope and your happiness again. You may not have experienced the death of a child before, and this is all new to you.

How to handle grief is not in a handbook that floods from the heavens. You learn how to move through it from experience, just like on-the-job training, along with support from others who have gone through it. Moving through your loss does not just happen. I promise that it will take a conscious decision and dedicated effort to heal.

Your brain, heart, and body have experienced trauma, just like your body does when you fall and break a bone. If you leave the bone to heal on itself you may wind up with a misshapen arm or leg, one that you cannot use to pick up a grocery bag or walk. Similarly, unresolved grief impacts how you live the rest of your life.

Grief's Impact

Grief, when not processed, can and most likely will come out "sideways." Here's what I mean by that: Your relationships may fail due to uncontrolled anger. You may lose your job because your depression keeps you from going to work. Lack of income may lead to loss of housing. Anxiety and depression inhibit sleep. (Sleep aids in the healing process from trauma.) There may be health consequences that lead to heart attack, stroke, obesity, diabetes, and much more. These things may not immediately surface. It may take years. Over time anger, shock, confusion, and guilt can build up and implode your life.

There are multiple physical symptoms of grief. Be in tune with your body. Is it telling you something? Are you feeling things differently that were not present before this happened? Ask yourself the following questions. (This is not an all-inclusive list. You may be experiencing other symptoms.)

- Do you feel fatigued and exhausted all the time? Are you constantly ready for a nap? After sleeping for the night, do you still feel tired?
- Do you have more aches and pains than usual? Do you feel like you have the flu, and it just will not go away? Grief can exacerbate pain.

- Are you having more headaches? Stress contributes to headaches, and you are now in a stressful season.
- Are you losing your keys and cell phone or do not remember what you were saying? This is common due to a shortened attention span.
- Do you have difficulty eating? Are you binging on sugary sweets? Is your stomach upset?
- Have you had more colds, coughs, or fevers? With stress comes a weakened immune system.
- Do you have difficulty breathing? The emotion of grief is associated with lung function. It constrains the lungs and the ability to expand and contract them.
- Do you have God or your higher power that you no longer trust?
- Do you blame God for what happened?
- Have you lost your sense of purpose?

It Is About Choices

I believe in choices and self-responsibility. What you think, how you act, and how you respond to life is totally up to you. Do not blame anyone for your choices and the results. This concept may be a bit difficult to digest right now, so allow me to explain. We all go through tough circumstances. Believe me, I've had more than my fair share. I could sit and wallow in self-pity or decide to make the most of the circumstances that have been handed to me. I am not happy about what has happened. There are some things I just cannot change.

May you find comfort in knowing you are not alone on this journey; other parents have gone through the same thing. They have survived. They have found joy. They live without guilt. What you decide to do with your new norm is up to you.

One of the biggest fears of a parent after their loss is that their child will be forgotten. In your attempt to hold on to your memories, you may be reluctant to step out of the darkness. I guarantee your child will not be forgotten. In the beginning, it may be difficult to think about your child without buckets of tears. That is normal. Tears are healing. They help to express your emotions. Looking at pictures of your child can help you move through your grief. Memories cannot be taken away. Those memories will help you to heal.

Hold on to them, but not too tightly. This is what I know is true. The tighter you hold on to those memories, the less you will be able to remember. Think of it this way, when you have a handful of groceries, there is only so much you can hold. When you put them down, store them in their proper place, you have room to pick up more. Each time you do this, your groceries are safely deposited in your kitchen. This is just like your memories. I suggest you write down all the reminiscences that pop into your head to make space for more remembrances to be jogged. Each time you do this memory dump onto paper, you preserve that specific recollection while allowing your brain to recall a new set of them.

It is easy to see only darkness with the loss of a child. It is a natural reaction. In times of trouble, it is difficult to be grateful on any level. I totally understand if you find it challenging to be grateful for anything at this point in your life. One of the things I do is write what I am grateful for on a small sticky note and place it in a gratitude jar. Examples of my gratitude are simple. I am grateful for my warm bed. I am grateful for the sunshine. I am grateful for a hot shower. I am grateful that I am healthy. I am grateful for spring.

That simple act of acknowledging good things helps to turn my thinking from desperation to joy. It works. It works in our subconscious mind by telling our conscious brain to see the good things, even in difficult circumstances. It is what I do with my current situation that counts.

Above all, be gentle with yourself. Give yourself permission to grieve and permission to heal. This is a journey, and it will take twists and turns with ups and downs. Grief may happen at the grocery store, on the phone, or at the gym. Give yourself permission to be happy. Lose your guilt over happiness. Your child would want you to move forward. This experience has changed you. You cannot deny it. There is no going back. Be open to the new chapter in your life. It can either be written without your approval or with it.

Grief on Your Terms

As a loss traveler, you will come to understand that grief is individualized. Learn that you can grieve on your terms. I have survived the loss of two children. Most recently it was my twenty-four-year-old son who passed away. Upon the breaking news of his death, I had dozens of people tell me what I should be doing and how to grieve. I was flooded with text messages, emails, and Facebook messages on what books to read, what groups to attend, and what to believe. I was so touched by the outpouring of caring and love, yet at the same time I felt overwhelmed. I sincerely thanked each person who offered advice.

I kept their recommendations in a folder "for later" if I ever needed or wanted them. What upset me, though, was that several people were offended when I told them I was not ready for their suggestions. I even had one friend become indignant with me and insist that I follow her advice. I politely told her that I was not ready and that, if the time came, I would check it out. Not only was I dealing with the loss of a child but was now being told how to grieve for him. This was a double whammy that I did not want to deal with.

Nevertheless, I know every single one of those friends was well-intentioned, and their advice came from their heartfelt desire to help. I decided my grief journey would be on my terms, my way, and with a process and tools that work for me.

With that being said, my process does not have to be your process. Nothing is being imposed on you. You came here looking for help, and that is precisely what I wish for you. But you choose. You can choose to take it all, take a little, or take none of it at all. Most importantly, all the experiences, tools, and insights I share in this book are meant to support you, so you can move through your grief and heal. There is hope of peace, joy, and happiness once again.

Who Taught You How to Grieve?

As a young child, I did not learn how to grieve or mourn. When we visited my grandparents, we drove by a cemetery, and I would duck in the backseat, so I would not see the graves while holding my breath until we passed by. I can explain the hiding because cemeteries scared me, however, I cannot find a reason for holding my breath other than the fact that I was young and did not understand death. Maybe if I breathed the air from the cemetery I would die? Today I can laugh about it, but as a young child my fear was real. I was little and had no experience with death and dying. We did not talk about it in my house.

How we view death and dying impacts how we grieve. In the United States today, death is primarily understood through the language and concepts of medicine, which focus on treatment, recovery, and cure. Most Americans are not taught how to grieve.

Since the beginning of time, grieving was passed down through traditions and culture. Elders of tribes, matriarchs and patriarchs of families, and rulers of nations were the role models for younger generations. They taught rituals and customs to help those who were grieving. Those traditions provided a set of directions that added structure to a time of change and confusion.

This included answering questions about how to care for someone as they approached death, the moment of death, and after they died. Many cultures passed down specific rituals regarding how to handle a person's body after they died. Ancient traditions also guided whether you grieved publicly, privately, loudly, or quietly as well as how you supported one another. The specific guidelines are not the major factor. Rather, it is the fact that grieving was taught, and that death was viewed as just another aspect of life.

As a result, people of generations long before you have lived through loss. They had unspoken rules to help each other. It was a community. I would even say it was a large, possibly very large, extended family. They bore witness to your loss. They understood your pain. You did not walk the loss journey alone.

Once you learned how to navigate and live through death, you became one more person to teach your friends and family how to live after loss. You could now pass this knowledge down to future generations.

That was then. This is now. In the 21st century that has changed.

I believe as a culture we have lost the ability to teach new generations how to grieve. Rituals around death, dying, and grieving are rare. Who was your role model? Who taught you how to grieve? Did you receive help without asking for it? Who was there to support you?

Remember, grieving is not meant to be done in isolation. Form that community, link arms and support each other, so they feel your love, understanding, and grace. As a fellow grieving mother, please remember that we are all in this together.

CHAPTER 2

MY STORY

The subject of losing a child is unfathomable. I belong to a club that I never asked to join. I was forced into it. Blindsided and left to fend for myself. No one else I knew was in this club. It seemed like an exclusive club. And people were not clamoring to get into it. This club is called "child loss." There is darkness to this club that outsiders do not want to talk about. However, I, Peggy Green, do want to talk about it.

Phone Call Number One

My daughter Courtney was only nine months old when she died. It was a horrible accident. The morning she died it was her dad's day to take her to daycare. She was crying when I left for work. I gave her a big hug and put her back in her crib. That was the last time I saw her alive. Courtney was starting to scooch across the floor. In no time she would be rolling around, then walking. She was a beautiful ball of joy. Her hair was a fuzzy blond and looked so much like her Grandpa Green's hair. She loved to go on walks in her stroller and be outdoors.

I received a call at work that something was wrong with her, and I needed to get to the hospital as soon as possible. This was before cell phones. I called my parents and asked them to meet me at the hospital, because I could not get in touch with Jesse. It was rush hour. The police insisted I have a coworker drive me. My coworker drove like a madman to get me there. He snuck through lines at stoplights, went down the side of the highway, and drove over the speed limit. After what seemed hours, we pulled into the emergency room driveway.

As we pulled up, I saw my dad and another man waiting for us. As soon as I got out of the car and came close enough to the man, I saw his nametag. It said Chaplain. It was then I knew Courtney was dead. Dad confirmed my biggest fear. Courtney was dead. I was ushered into a room where my mom sat with tears streaming down her face. I ran and fell into her arms. The three of us, Mom, Dad, and I, hugged. It was horrible. My head was spinning. How? She was at the babysitter's house. The babysitter loved Courtney.

I still had not managed to reach Jesse at that point. He was working as a salesman and was not in the office. It was his night to pick Courtney up from the sitter. I frantically called all his buddies to see if they knew where he was. No one knew. One was even joking with me, and in my desperation to find Jesse, I yelled, "Courtney is dead! Where is Jesse?" I am known for being pretty direct, and this got the point across. While I was tracking down Jesse, the police were at the babysitter's house. They were waiting for Jesse to pick up Courtney.

When he showed up, they directed him to the hospital. We met at the hospital in that tiny room with other family members who gathered.

I asked to see Courtney. I was told it would not be pretty. I did not care. I had to see her. I had to make it real. It was ugly. Her tiny body lying on the table. It was cold. It was sterile. In my grief and desperation, I yelled at her, "Courtney, wake up!" I knew it was not going to happen, but we do crazy things in grief. Unbeknownst to me, this would not be the first of many of my insane thoughts or actions. Grief does weird things to the way we think and act.

Phone Call Number Two

Connor is my only son. At twenty-four years old, he was growing into a fine young man. He was patient and kind. He was the kind of guy who would do anything to help someone else, even to his detriment. Connor would help others move, risking being late for work because his friends were more important.

Connor was a good young man, however, he struggled with the common things that many young adults are doing their best to figure out. He was working through finances, relationships, and career.

He chose sobriety over drugs for many years. One of the basic tenets of 12-step recovery groups is to give back by volunteering. Without money-management experience, he volunteered as the treasurer for one of his weekly meetings. He felt an obligation to give back to the community that helped him in his sobriety. He also gave back by sponsoring his peers to help them work through their program. He was a teacher and a friend.

He loved dogs and rescued Mac. He is a beautiful mix of Labrador, pit bull, and St. Bernard. Imagine big, playful, and stubborn. Mac had terrible behavior. I remember encouraging Connor to return Mac to the pound. He was too much work, too hard to handle. Connor would not hear of it. He took it upon himself to train Mac. Through time and effort, Mac became a well-behaved companion. He loved walks, playing with other dogs, and lying next to Connor as he played games on Xbox.

My son was a great kid. He made some mistakes in his life but nothing that could not be fixed. Connor loved to skateboard. He received a skateboard for Christmas when he was about nine years old. Once he got his feet on it there was no stopping him. He learned to "do stairs," flip his board, ride ramps, and ride the rails. I remember watching him teach a young boy at the skate park. He showed patience with others. He had no fear. He was not afraid of getting hurt. He had a heart for others.

Connor loved his family. We shared the love of dogs, hiking, and the mountains. We also talked about business, and the importance of making customers happy and helping them realize their dreams. We talked the same language.

Whenever we had family gatherings for holidays or special events, Connor always invited his friends. He knew we would make it work, we would make room for an extra chair at the table. We would make room for one more. That saying, "room for one more" is now his legacy.

Connor took responsibility for his actions. He knew his decisions were his. He was that young man who did not blame anyone for his life circumstances.

On December 14, 2018, in the midst of rush-hour traffic, I answered a phone call from a number I did not recognize. It was my oldest daughter, Brittany. She said, "Mom." Then I heard her say to another person, "I know he hasn't been feeling well lately." My mother's instinct told me to get off the highway. Then nothing. Silence. She did not respond to me when I called her name. By now my stomach was flipping. I knew she was talking about her brother, my son Connor. They worked together at car dealerships next to each other. It was common that they were together, helping each other.

I hung up and called her back on her private cell phone. Brittany told me in a shaky, barely audible voice, "Mom, I don't know how to tell you this, but Connor is dead. He killed himself." My heart stopped. I shouted out at the top of my lungs: "Nooooo!" How could this be? Connor, my only son. Dead? Why? How? All the questions came flooding in.

I immediately got back on the highway and called a friend. She told me to come pick her up, and she would go with me to see my son. I was shaking. I was in tears. I was crying out to God. Why? Why? Why?

What happened next is a blur. I do not remember the exact details. This is what I do recall. I picked up my friend, and it was an excruciating ride in bumper-to-bumper traffic to get across town to see my son, my daughters, and my niece. My youngest daughter, Hannah, was on that side of town and beat me to the dealership. My niece's business is on that side of town. She beat me there. Connor's dad even beat me there.

When I got to Connor's work, I ran in to hug my girls. I vaguely remember shouting "No. No. No. Why? Why? Why? How can this be?" The police were already there. They had started their investigation. After what seemed like forever, we were asked if we wanted to see Connor. Yes, I had to! I felt that if I did not see him, it would not be real. I was reliving having to see Courtney. It was all a bad dream. I said yes.

Brittany, my friend, and I went around the corner to see Connor. He looked as if he was asleep. I knelt beside him and just looked at him. I was terrified to touch him. I felt Brittany's eyes on the back of my head. I met my friend's eyes as I knelt next to my son. Her eyes were filled with tears and compassion. I felt the police officers watching me. I was afraid they would yell at me if I touched him. It was now a crime scene. Even though it was evident it was suicide, they needed to confirm no foul play. An autopsy had to be completed. Connor had to be taken to the police morgue. I was not leaving until he was picked up and taken away.

Those hours were the longest of my life, waiting and waiting. I watched in shock as my son was taken away on a gurney in a black body bag. It was surreal. It was like the movies. However, this time, it was not an empty bag filled to look like a human, it was my son. I could not believe this was happening.

Family Losses

My father passed away in 1999. He was only sixty-nine years old. He was my mentor. He was the one who taught me to have goals. He taught me to take care of myself. He taught me how to wire a ceiling light. He taught me about finances. He taught me how to garden and to love the outdoors. He was that positive male figure.

Dad was fighting cancer and announced to the family that he was discontinuing the chemotherapy. He was done. He did not like the way he felt. This upset the entire family, especially my older sister,

Penny, who wanted him to keep fighting. She hated his decision. She hated him for not trying to beat his cancer. However, after he stopped the chemotherapy, he had quality of life. He was able to get out of bed, eat his meals at the table, and get outdoors into his garden. The garden was his place to go to think, harvest from the earth, and be peaceful.

I read *The Catcher in the Rye* out loud to him in his final week. We always talked about reading it together but had never gotten around to it. I read it. He listened. I know he heard me even though he could not tell me. It was the last father-daughter thing we did together.

When the time came, we were all by my dad's side when he passed. He looked around and took inventory of his family who came to say goodbye. Once everyone was present, he took his last breath. It was done. He was out of pain. That was in 1999.

My sister, Penny, passed away from lung cancer ten years after Dad passed away. She was only fifty-three years old. This was a deja vu moment. Her cancer surfaced after a stressful time in her life. My sister was my best friend. We were five years apart, and after Courtney died, she helped bring me to God.

Penny was an awesome sister. We loved to play softball, scrapbook, and talk on the phone for hours. Our favorite pastime was our annual baking day. We would get together to bake cookies, dozens of them, in multiple varieties. We kept our heritage going by baking Swedish tea rings, a wonderful bread with brown sugar, cinnamon, and walnuts. Our mom taught us how to do that and the ladies of the house got together to carry on the tradition every year. My sister taught me love, compassion, and to stand up for myself. I miss her horribly, and nobody, nobody can replace her.

Family death has become a part of my life. My mom passed away in 2016 from lung cancer — a third person in my family to die from cancer. May I just say, cancer sucks. Mom was eighty-four years old. She endured a long battle with poor health, lack of quality of life, and multiple illnesses. Mom wore her heart on her sleeve. She worried about all of us. She wanted the best for us. She helped us when we were down. Mom outlived Dad, something I thought would never happen. I love my mom. I see myself in her. I see her in me.

Mom was ready to move on. Her life was miserable. I often joked with her, "If you were a horse, we would have taken you out of your pain years ago." She understood. We have more empathy for an animal that suffers than for a human who suffers. I share this because it is me. It is how I think. I voice my opinion and am not afraid to be judged by others. It is important that I am able to be who I am.

Walking the Rope Bridge of Grief

When my son died, I had no idea how I was going to survive, how I was going to make it through the day, let alone the next month or years to come. I remember that pain and fear so vividly. It was horrible. I was moving through life as if I were a robot. I was numb yet still felt deep sadness and anguish.

At some point, I do not recall exactly when it happened, I found that in the present I needed help so I could have hope for the future.

I compare my journey to that of traversing a rope bridge, one of those pedestrian foot bridges that hangs over a deep gorge with a rushing river below. They are usually suspended hundreds of feet above the water and anchored into the cliff walls. There are no pillars to support the middle, and the arc of the bridge deepens with the weight of the person walking upon it.

The rope bridge I imagine is constructed of rope and planks. It uses the bare minimum of materials with gaps at your feet and simple rope handrails, exposing you to the perils below. The bridge and anyone walking over it are subjected to wind, rain, hail, heat, and cold.

Although it is a precarious walk, the bridge is a crossing to neighboring villages that support one another with food, supplies, community, and connection. It is passage from one area to another that otherwise would not be accessible.

I wanted to be on the other side of the deep gorge of sadness and grief. I was suspended between my current reality and the reality of what could be. Crossing the rope bridge, constructed by others who had experienced the tragedy of child death, was my ticket to healing. It was important that I sought help from others to overcome the pain and stay positive.

On one side of the bridge, I stood with my present circumstances of deep pain, and on the other side I could see hope and joy. I had the ashes of mourning and could see the beauty of the future. I believe my higher power is a healer, but I was stressed, frustrated, and incredibly sad. I wanted to receive the oil of joy yet had difficulty imagining joy again. I wanted to overcome my fear and have hope for the future. I yearned to turn my pain into purpose.

How did I do it when I was experiencing these diametrical emotions? The bridge seemed impassable. Fear started to take over when I thought about taking a step onto the bridge. Would I make it? The prospect of falling existed with every step.

I could focus on the possibility of slipping on a weather-worn plank, or that it could break without warning, sending me to the depths of despair, helplessness, and depression. Or I could set my sights on the other side of the bridge where hope, joy, and purpose awaited me. I chose the latter.

I realized I could not get across the bridge, move forward, without taking the first step. Somehow, I had to navigate those perilous planks, the unsure footing, the side-to-side swaying, the unsettling rise and fall of the bridge. I was placed at this crossroads without my permission. I knew that the joy I was robbed of would return. It was there — in the future.

When I saw myself in the middle of the bridge, I looked back and realized the desperation had lessened, and I began to experience joy. I focused on the other side of the bridge, which offered purpose, and everything I did took me one step closer. It did not happen overnight. I learned patience with myself and waited expectantly for healing. I held out for hope.

Every day I took a deep breath to move forward. I also trusted in myself and the necessity of the process. I leaned into others who had gone through child loss before me, lived to tell about it, and rediscovered joy. They navigated the rope bridge of grief and healing, encouraging me to do the same.

My grief journey does not end once on the other side. However, my pain has eased with time.

I Am a Survivor

In the span of thirty years, I have lost two children, both parents, and a sister and have gone through a divorce. That does not even count in-laws, nieces, and cousins who have gone before me. This story is about how I survived my losses, how resiliency has helped, and how my optimism moves me forward.

When I share my story, I am often told, "You have been through a lot." When I look at it from other people's perspectives, I guess you could say that I have been through a lot. I have come to accept that this is my norm. My life includes the death of children, parents, and siblings.

It has been important for me to be able to acknowledge the magnitude of my losses. This book is about how I survived loss — how I moved through the grief process to discover hope and healing — and how you can too. I am often asked how I have made it through my life this far with all this trauma and tragedy. Reflecting back on it, it has been my perseverance, my desire to live a full life, and my commitment to use the tools I acquired over the years.

Courtney was the first in this series of family deaths. The pain is less. I still think about her, even more so since Connor passed. With each death, I acquired new tools to lean on to conquer the grief. One tool is my ability to focus on having a purpose to live. Who am I living for? Who am I helping? I find when I take the focus off myself, my grief, my pain lessens. My circumstances are no worse than others nor any better. It makes me realize that I can be grateful for what I have. My purpose has changed over time. My purpose is now to help others work through their grief and be happy again.

In fact, my purpose has morphed dramatically in the last three years. This is where I am now: "My purpose in life is to be joyful, grateful, present, encouraging, positive, be the best possible version of myself in my personal and professional relationships, and exemplify Christ in all I do so that I am an example of life's possibilities."

Learning How to Grieve

Death is often perceived as a failure of the medical system and talking about it makes many folks uncomfortable. Grief is frequently seen as an individual problem. It no longer is part of the culture to support others who are grieving. Bereavement is viewed as a medical crisis to be resolved, and normal grieving behaviors are sometimes interpreted as symptoms of a psychiatric or medical condition. For much of the twentieth century, our understanding of grief was built primarily on the psychoanalytic theories of Sigmund Freud. Mourners were often told to "put the past behind you," "get back to normal," and "move on."

Plus, we look at death as losing and being alive as winning. When we look at the language around death — for example, "he lost his battle to cancer" — we often use sports terms. We apply terms about competition to life and death when really, of course, death is not losing and being alive is not winning.

Most likely you were not taught how to process and feel the pain of grief. The truth is that you cannot heal what you do not feel. Do not cancel out the future by staying focused on the past. Life goes on. Grief erases normalcy. Arrive at a new normal.

So, while there is no timeline to grief, there are certain markers you can use to help you know where you are in the process of grieving.

Grief is often described as a journey, one that will never end. However, healing does happen. The grief becomes more manageable.

How do you know if you are moving forward? While you are going through grief it is difficult to see progress.

Change and improvement happen over time. Grief is different for everyone. Growth is subtle, and without having an awareness of it you may miss that it is even happening at all.

If you are intentional with your healing and being an active participant, you can learn to recognize the changes in attitude and behavior in order to measure progress on your journey.

My Toolbox

Just like my mom, I am vulnerable and openly share my feelings. I wear my heart on my sleeve. I let others see who I am. I am not afraid to tell someone, "I love you." I cry in public. If someone asks why the tears, I share that I am crying because I miss my son. After Connor's death, I started blogging my thoughts on Facebook. My readers saw how my heart ached, but they also saw how I dealt with my pain. I started to express my fears, doubts, and dreams. It was not just the bad things. I found that sharing the good is equally important. Being vulnerable has helped in my loss journey.

Twelve-step recovery programs have added tools to my toolbox. I first started taking part in Al-Anon meetings in 1998. Al-Anon is a partner program for friends and family of alcoholics. I began attending because I was at a loss as to what to do. My marriage was in trouble. The biggest takeaway at the time was to trust in your higher power. It was a long time coming, but the pieces came together for my God. My sister Penny stuck with me, and it was time to release everything to God. This was about the same time that Dad was starting his health challenges. Al-Anon brought me to my God and helped me to navigate my relationship with Jesse.

I had another opportunity to tap into a twelve-step program when both Brittany and Connor entered Cornerstone, an alcohol and drug recovery program for youth. I participated in the parent companion twelve-step program and learned many more valuable tools. One of those tools is to "take what you like and leave the rest." With this principle, you may not like everything you hear and read. You may like only one or two ideas that you can apply in your circumstances. That is what it means. Take the parts you like, apply them, or keep them for later use, and leave the rest.

Here's an example. What happens behind the scenes of entrepreneurship is more than I signed up for. I started my entrepreneurial career because I wanted to help others as a personal trainer. (This was prior to my current work as a grief coach, speaker, and author.) I wanted to make a difference in people's health and wellness. I did not know I would have to learn so many new skills. I returned to college to gain the skills as a personal trainer. I learned about muscle groups, heart rates, metabolism, and nutrition. I learned how to write great workouts for weight loss and strength gains. I learned how to work with different populations: pregnant women, seniors, youth, and everyone in between.

What I did not learn was how to build a business. Basic business-building skills I needed included marketing and developing client relationships. I had to believe in myself and believe in my company. I intentionally sought ways to learn those skills. I have been blessed with fantastic business and personal development mentors. I have worked with multiple coaches and participated in numerous seminars. I was introduced to a wide variety of ideas and often found that I would "take what I liked and leave the rest."

To this day, I use many of the tools and techniques I acquired throughout my business and personal life, and I find the opportunity to learn something new daily. This gives me the chance to add to my grief recovery toolbox, so I am better equipped to help others. I never understood the power of these tools outside of my business until Connor passed. However, unknowingly at first, I have been tapping into them for years.

When I take a look at what has enabled me to survive my losses and be able to move forward, it is how I live my life. I grew up spending hours playing outdoors with neighbors, participating in sports, and communing with nature. I discovered at a young age how good I felt when I was outdoors. I enjoyed running and knew the positive impact it had on me. Even when I attended college and experienced stress, I made sure I got outdoors.

My life journey also incorporates awareness of self-care that includes exercise, proper nutrition, sleep, water, and mental health. Since Courtney's death, I have grown in my spiritual journey. Since that fateful day in 1991, I have grown tremendously. My faith is what rounds me out as the person I am today. It is with great pleasure that I will be sharing how restoring these four areas — physical, mental, emotional, and spiritual health — have assisted in my grief process and can help you as well.

Today, I find joy in every day. Honestly, some days are a struggle, but I work on it. The journey has changed me. I fondly remember my sister, parents, and children. I have several reasons to live. I have two beautiful daughters, a grandson, and a granddaughter. I am now the matriarch of my family, and I do not take it lightly.

CHAPTER 3

INTRODUCING THE THREE PHASES TO MOVE THROUGH GRIEF TO HEALING

This book was written for people just like you. You may feel stuck in your grief or feel that you do not have the tools and resources to move forward. However, you want to move through your grief to healing.

This pain has been forced upon you; you did not have a say in it. But the journey you are about to embark upon *is* your choice. A journey of healing is never an easy one. I do promise that if you are open to the journey, things can and will change and get better. What is on the other side of that rope bridge is hope, peace, and joy. It is a journey that never ends. It just gets less bumpy.

The alternative is a sorry state of living. I do not say that to scare you. It is a reality check. I say it because it is the truth. I have seen it happen. I have seen parents, relationships, and marriages destroyed by the loss of a child. Do not let the death of your child dictate your happiness for the rest of your life.

I will say this time and time again — I am offering the tools that helped me move forward on my loss journey. The Three Phases to Move through Grief to Healing comes from experience. I believe someone like myself who has life experience versus formal specialized college training and certifications can be the best person to walk beside you in a tough season. Congratulations on taking a big step. It is not easy to recognize or admit that you can use some help.

Each part in the Three Phases does not work in isolation. They overlap, and you will probably visit each one multiple times. I found that depending on where I was in my grief process, there was a tool that was much more relevant and useful in the moment. Tap into the tools as you deem necessary. There is no right or wrong order. I encourage you to read the entire book and come back and reference it often. Remember, you can take what you like and leave the rest.

If you have a print copy of this book, highlight what is important, write in the margins your thoughts, or dog-ear the pages. If you are reading it digitally, I suggest you have a notebook to write down notes. There is an abundance of useful information that will help you heal. When you need a specific tool, the last thing you want to do is search for answers. Keep them at your fingertips.

With each step, a new set of emotions may surface, or it may be some of the same old ones. Either way, going through these phases will support you in facing those emotions. Emotions come out wherever you are. It is good to learn to cope with them instead of sweeping them under the rug. You will find out more about yourself than you ever imagined. You have been changed by the loss of your child, and you now have the chance to grow, be better, and make a difference. You will have the courage and strength to face your emotions and face what lies ahead.

The Three Phases are meant to ease the grieving process. Stepping through these phases will not entirely take away the pain. Intentionally work through the phases. Put into action what you learn. When you are amidst a grief wave, you will have tools to utilize. You will have resources available at your fingertips. Learn them. Use them. Practice them. They will support you.

Since my son passed in 2018, I have helped thousands with my *Thursday Thoughts*, multiple podcast appearances, speaking on suicide, and working one-on-one with coaching clients.

The Three Phases to Move through Grief to Healing process has ten parts. These came together as I have been going through my recent loss journey and guiding others in theirs. The Three Phases is a melting pot of tools and resources that have helped me. Some are tried and true while others are new. I can say they work together. You may find one piece more useful than another. I am okay with that. I am thrilled to share with you what worked for me.

Joanne's Story

The first person I worked with as a grief coach was my friend, Joanne. She shared that she had given up on life. She was no longer making herself a priority. She saw her health decline, saw her depression deepen, and was no longer happy. She did not like the decisions she was making. She found she was not living the life she wanted.

Joanne lost a nephew in a car accident several years before. He was her favorite nephew, and they were close. They did so much together. She was helping him study for his college entrance exams. He wanted to attend the same college she did. He helped her with chores around her house, and they both had a love for techno concerts. I understood why she was grieving and also told her that she could find the same happiness she had prior to his death.

We spent some time talking about her choices and the consequences, both positive and negative. Initially, she felt as if she was handling the loss of her nephew quite well. She became a workaholic and spent less time at home with her husband and children. When she was home, she was in her home office working late into the night, missed meals with her family, and was at the office before anyone was up.

She recognized that she was hiding behind her work. She did not want to face the reality of her nephew's death. She was angry with the man who had caused the accident. She was not able to talk about it. She stuffed all her emotions and feelings. Taking a closer look at her behavior, she realized she was not dealing with the loss at all.

I told her about Courtney and Connor, what I was doing to move through my grief, and how it was working for me. I shared with her that even though it was one of the most difficult things I had ever done, I accepted that Connor was gone. He was no longer living on this earth. The chasm I felt with Courtney and Connor's deaths was being bridged by my attitude and perseverance. I told her that I was not looking for perfection, rather for progress. I knew she could do the same. She had a choice to make.

Joanne expressed her desire to rediscover her relationship with her husband and children. She decided to stop taking on extra work, leave her work at the office, and set aside time to be with her family. She also started writing down her goals. She now had the time and purpose to move forward. She did not feel like she was dishonoring her nephew but rather honoring him. Living a fulfilling life is something he would have wanted her to do.

The following paragraphs introduce my process: Three Phases to Move through Grief to Healing. You will learn much more about this process — and how it can help you — throughout this book. Use the Three Phases to guide you in discovering a purpose to move forward. Remember that you are not alone on this voyage. I share my stories to demonstrate you can not only survive this journey, but you can thrive. If I can do it, you can do it. Your story is different. It is unique. However, the Three Phases will work for you too. There is hope, and I believe in you. You can regain joy after losing your child.

Take my hand, and let us do this together.

The Three Phases to Move through Grief to Healing are: Acceptance, Overcome Your Fear, and Recovery. As you move through the phases, you will learn to live with the loss of your loved one and be able to find your new norm.

Within each phase there are three or four parts. I will take you through each of these three phases while diving deeper into each part. The following paragraphs offer a brief introduction of these phases, which will guide you from grief to healing.

THREE PHASES TO MOVE
THROUGH GRIEF TO HEALING

Phase I — Acceptance
Part 1: Understand Your Grief
Part 2: Permission to Grieve
Part 3: Permission to Heal

Phase II — Overcome Your Fear
Part 1: Understand Your Fear
Part 2: Identify Your Fear
Part 3: Face Your Fear

Phase III — Recovery
Part 1: Physical Health
Part 2: Mental Health
Part 3: Emotional Health
Part 4: Spiritual Health

Phase I — Acceptance

I know this to be true. Once you are able to accept your loss, you will be able to move forward in your healing. It is necessary to accept that your loved one is gone, so you can and will heal. Acceptance is a process that offers hope and inspiration, eventually more frequently, and longer over a period of time. Acceptance does not mean forgetting. It does mean being able to move forward.

Part 1: Acceptance — Understand Your Grief

You will identify what grief is and assess what type of grief you are experiencing. Understanding your grief will help you move through it to healing.

Part 2: Acceptance — Permission to Grieve

You will learn that it is okay to grieve and, more importantly, you will give yourself permission to do so.

Part 3: Acceptance — Permission to Heal

You will learn how to give yourself permission to heal. You will feel better knowing you are not alone with this experience of grief as a result of losing your child. You will accept your grieving experience as valid and no longer deny yourself what you need.

Phase II — Overcome Your Fear

The fear of pain of healing may have you completely paralyzed, stuck, and unable to move forward. I will help you to identify your fear then face it, so you are free to take the next steps on your loss journey. Your fear and pain will not last forever.

Part 1: Overcome Your Fear — Understand Your Fear

You will learn about five types of fear. You may experience multiple types of fear throughout your grief journey. You will understand the impact fear has on your ability to move through grief to healing.

Part 2: Overcome Your Fear — Identify Your Fear

You will be looking at the source of your fears by doing some self-evaluation and asking pertinent questions to gently guide you to self-discovery. Here we will also focus on what it takes to get through one day at a time. Be open to challenging your negative thoughts. Finally, with the facts in hand, you will be able to take the next step to face those fears.

Part 3: Overcome Your Fear — Face Your Fear

Now that you know what fears trip you up, you will learn ways to fight those fears. Walking through your specific fears will allow you to act. You will have tools to draw upon, consequently learning from experience to discover what works and what does not work for you. You will be equipped to face your fears when they arise.

PHASE III — RECOVERY

Recovery is healing physical, mental, emotional, and spiritual health. Your pain and suffering caused by the death of your child impact all areas of your health. You will learn how these four areas of health are related to each other just like the pieces of a jigsaw puzzle. When one piece is missing, the picture is unfinished. The same with your grief recovery. If healing is missed in one area of health, then your recovery is incomplete.

Part 1: Recovery — Physical Health

You will learn about the association of taking care of yourself physically in healing your grief. We will talk about a wide variety of self-care strategies and techniques that you can use.

Part 2: Recovery — Mental Health

You will learn about the narratives you tell yourself and how they impact your ability to move forward. You will come to understand how to rewrite the stories you tell yourself and use the new ones to help you see circumstances in a new and positive light.

Part 3: Recovery — Emotional Health

You will learn that emotions are automatic responses, and it is important to feel them and experience them. Through thinking differently, you will be equipped to change the way you respond to situations, thus helping you to experience good feelings.

Part 4: Recovery — Spiritual Health

You will identify what spirituality is for you and some indicators of healthy spirituality. Spiritual health is a personal matter involving values, integrity, and compassion that support the purpose and mission of your life. You get to decide what spirituality looks like.

Death and loss are part of the circle of life and a painful reality. It is guaranteed to happen to everyone at some time. People react to it uniquely, and the effects may remain for months or years. It is your response to your loss that impacts your ability to live a fulfilling and productive life. You have a choice. Listen to what your body needs. Listen to what your soul needs.

"Wholistic" Grief Healing

I consider my Three Phases to Move through Grief to Healing to be a "wholistic" process, because it is founded on restoring your physical, mental, emotional, and spiritual health. Plus, you have probably already realized that this is not your traditional psychological, counseling book written by a therapist, psychologist, or psychiatrist. I am a grief coach, and there is a difference between coaching and therapy. A counselor focuses on the past, helping the griever to explore unresolved feelings they have with their relationship with the loved one who has passed away.

Most mourners are open to moving through grief, sometimes oscillating between feelings of sorrow and pleasure even from the earliest weeks of loss. It is natural, in other words, to experience happiness and sadness at the same time — to look forward with hope even as you look backward to reflect and grieve.

Coaching reinforces this resilience by helping you forge a positive vision for the future. As a grief coach, I focus on the future and help you get back up on your feet, find your new norm, and encourage personal growth through loss. I also focus on taking action, helping you to be an active participant in your healing. You learn to change behaviors and improve the way you think about your life. As a coach I help you find your own path to healing. I guide you through unfamiliar territory by talking with you and helping you understand what you are experiencing.

Instead of looking back at what was, I am here to ensure you focus on what is ahead of you. A death, whether sudden or expected, will turn your world upside down and leave you lost with no idea how to navigate your changed life. Yes, it is a changed life, but it is still one that you need to live.

It is important not to get stuck in a bad place. With compassion and understanding I help you to move forward and create a vision for your future without your loved one while still holding them dear to your heart.

Coaches help you process your feelings, but the goal is to look ahead. You are still alive and have a future to plan. Loss may change your future, and the grief coach shows you how to adapt.

Think about how your loss does not have to define you but how it can *refine* you. This example might make sense to you. I can define myself as Connor's mom, or I can define myself as a mother of four who is living a happy, joy-filled life. I am also doing something I would not be doing had Connor not ended his life. I am helping others on their grief journey and grateful that I can do so.

I do this now because no mother should have to go through this alone. Over thirty years ago, with the loss of my daughter, I had extraordinarily little support. Talking about her was taboo, and there were no grief support groups.

Today I compress fourteen years of fitness education, nutrition consulting, and wellness with thirty years of personal experience to write this book. Having directly used the tools and resources, I know they work. They are 100 percent responsible for me being here today and helping you.

The Three Phases to Move through Grief to Healing process and specific tools presented in this book are intended to open your mind to possibilities, see life differently, and ultimately guide you to move from grief to healing. I highly recommend experiencing each and every one of these tools. You may be surprised to discover what they will do for you.

CHAPTER 4

———

UNDERSTANDING
SUICIDE

Y ou lost your child by suicide. Suddenly you are labeled as a
suicide loss survivor. It helps to know what that means. The
following definition will help: Anyone who is close to someone who died by suicide and feels affected is a suicide loss survivor.

With that being said, let's look at various aspects of suicide to
better understand it. The more you know, the better your healing.

Shocking and Surprising Statistics of Suicide

I found comfort in learning the facts and statistics of suicide.
Some of them are absolutely overwhelming. My heart goes out to the
millions of people who are suffering because of the suicide death of a
loved one. Here are facts and statistics from various online sources:

- Suicide is a major global health problem with 1,300,000 suicides in the world in 2020.
- Suicides increased by 66 percent worldwide from 2019 to 2020.
- There are currently over 47,000 suicides annually in the U.S.
- Suicide is the eleventh leading cause of death in the U.S., which is twice as many deaths as HIV/AIDS.
- There were more than twice as many suicides in the U.S. as there were homicides.
- Suicide is the second leading cause of death for people ages 10 to 34.
- Suicide is the fourth leading cause among people ages 34 to 54 and the fifth leading cause among people ages 45 to 54.
- Men have a higher suicide rate, but women have a higher attempt rate.
- Male suicide to female suicide is 4:1.
- Approximately 1 in 20 adolescents experience a suicide (friends or relatives) in 1 year and 1 in 5 before their adulthood.

What, Who, When, Where, How, and Why

After my son died, I started researching suicide. I wanted answers and found they provided some relief to my anguish. Through my online research and my own fact-finding mission, I found some answers. At least as much as I will ever get. I looked at all of Connor's Facebook messages, looked at his cell phone texts and pictures, and listened to his voicemail messages. I spent time talking with — more like interrogating — friends and family who were with him in the days and weeks before he passed. What did they see? What did he tell them? I spent months in this insane investigation mode. I wanted and demanded answers.

If you have done anything similar to what I just described, you are not alone. There are others who have gone down this road.

When I started putting my answers together, it was like I had run an intense investigation of a crime, looking for the what, who, when, where, how, and why. No stone was left unturned. However, there was still a mystery. You may find yourself in the same place. The answer to *why*. We will get to that in a few minutes. I feel it is important to know the rest of the story, because it helps with the *why*. The following explanations are based on my years of research, reading, and continuing investigation on this topic.

What is Suicide?

The Centers for Disease Control and Prevention's Facts About Suicide web page sheds light on suicide, suicide attempts, and suicidal ideation. According to the CDC:

- "Suicide is self-directed injurious behavior with intent to end your own life as a result of the behavior."
- "A suicide attempt is a non-fatal, self-directed, potentially injurious behavior with intent to die as a result of the behavior."
- "Suicidal ideation is when you think about, consider, or plan your own death."

Finally, I would like to add my personal belief: Suicide is not an act of selfishness, weakness, or cowardness.

Who Dies by Suicide?

It is our loved ones — brothers, fathers, sons, sisters, mothers, daughters, and grandparents — as well as friends and coworkers. It may be someone we love so deeply that the pain is unbearable. The risk of suicide varies greatly by age, sex, and race and by personal characteristics including education, occupation, family history, and place of residence. It can be the kid down the block trying to get through high school. It can be the dad working in the office or the daughter working on the factory floor. Suicide even takes young mothers and retired grandmothers.

The American Association of Suicidology reports that every death by suicide leaves behind at least 130 people who report they knew the person who died. Of those, it is likely at least a third (about forty-three people) feel remarkably close to the person who died and might need postvention (immediate help to promote healing). With nearly 50,000 suicides in the U.S. annually, this creates about two million people annually who are directly impacted by the suicide of someone close to them. I am sorry that you are part of this group.

These are some staggering statistics, would you not agree?

Simply put, suicide knows no boundaries. It does not discriminate with age, race, gender, country, region, or education. Suicide affects nearly everyone.

When Do Most Suicides Occur?

This might surprise you. We have been led to believe that suicide rates increase with holiday stress and during winter when days get shorter. Research shows the opposite. According to an article written by Marc Shapiro and published on the Johns Hopkins Medicine website on May 4, 2019, seasonal effects on suicide rates suggest that the prevalence of suicide is greatest during the spring and summer months. In 2016 — the most recent year for which U.S. data are available — the months with the highest average daily suicides were August and July. The previous year it was May, July, and March.

According to the 2019 article on the Johns Hopkins Medicine website, there is inconclusive research except that few suicides occur between 4:00 and 8:00 a.m. Other than that, there is no rhyme or reason to the time a person chooses to end their life. Regarding days of the week, suicides occur most frequently on Monday for both males and females and for most age groups.

Where Do Suicides Occur?

About three-quarters of suicide incidents occur at home. Most people (85 percent) die at the scene and never make it to the hospital (National Violent Injury Statistics System data). Suicide rates are highest in rural areas, in the West (excluding California) and, to a lesser extent, in parts of the South and northern New England.

There is a degree of romanticism around taking one's life at a popular tourist attraction where others have ended their life. It gives them a sense of connection to those who have died before them. These places have been coined as "suicide landmarks."

There are well-known locations throughout the world for taking one's life. According to an article published by *Best School Counseling* on January 4, 2013, these leading suicide landmarks are:

1. Aokigahara Forest — Mount Fuji, Japan
2. Golden Gate Bridge, San Francisco, California
3. Nanjing Yangtze River Bridge — Nanjing, Jiansu, China

How Does Suicide Occur? What Are The Methods Used?

In my research, the methods of suicide actually surprised me. Maybe it is because of the multiple suicide losses I have experienced or the means by which my son ended his life. The Suicide Prevention Resource Center's latest statistics (2020) offer insight into the means of suicide:

- Firearms are now used in more suicides than homicides, making it the fastest growing method, nearly 53 percent of all suicides.
- Next is hanging, suffocation, or strangulation, which compose 27 percent of suicides.
- Solid and liquid poisons or overdoses compose 9 percent.
- The balance of suicides is completed by non-drug poisoning, cutting/piercing, falls, jumping from high places or into fast-moving objects or fires, or intentionally crashing a motor vehicle.

Why of Suicide

Why? This is the million-dollar question. Why did my loved one take their life?

The following list includes potential reasons for their decision. Often, it is the result of long-term difficulties with thoughts, feelings,

or experiences that the individual feels they cannot bear any longer.
Among other things, a person contemplating suicide may feel:

- Sadness or grief
- Shame
- Worthlessness
- Intense guilt
- Rage or a desire to seek revenge
- That they are a burden to others
- That they have no worth or value
- That life is not worth living
- That they are trapped, either physically or emotionally
- That things will never get better
- Intense physical or emotional pain

Many factors can contribute to a person feeling this way. It may
be due to events happening in their life. Perhaps:

- The loss of a loved one
- Bullying, discrimination, or abuse
- The end of a relationship
- A major change in life circumstances such as divorce, unem-
  ployment, retirement, or homelessness
- Receiving a diagnosis of a life-changing illness
- Problems with money
- Being in prison
- Pregnancy or pregnancy loss
- Questioning one's sexual or gender identity in an environ-
  ment that is not accepting of this

- Certain cultural practices such as forced marriage
- Surviving a traumatic event

However, suicide does not always occur because of a specific life event, and not everyone who experiences these events will consider suicide. People respond to adversity in different ways.

More than likely, your child's suicide involved a combination of many of these events and feelings. Then one day, one small simple thing became the weight on your loved one's shoulder they could no longer bear. They felt the only choice was to end it all.

What we do know from those who have attempted suicide and were not successful is they were in a lot of pain, physically, mentally or both. All they wanted to do was end the pain. The choice was not to end their life. It was to end the pain, and they believed the only way they could end the pain was to end their life.

Why did your loved one commit suicide? The answer will not be revealed. You can guess and presume what the issues were. The fact is you will never know the 100 percent truth. Know that asking *why* is normal and that, at first, it may feel impossible to ever get beyond that question. But eventually you will find a way of thinking that you can live with or accept.

Why Didn't You See the Symptoms?

As I work with suicide loss survivors, many tell me they were blindsided by their loved one's decision to end their life. I felt the same after Connor died. Understandably, he was establishing a new routine because he recently moved. His new home was with long-time friends, his dog Mac was with him, and he was working a satisfying job. The latest work schedule was exciting and challenging. We texted back and forth about customer service, asking questions, and working with a mentor.

Connor worked in the building next to his sister, and they spent a lot of time together. She saw his happiness. His cousin also spent time with him. The last time we spoke, he told me he was looking forward to Christmas. He did not want presents. All he wanted was my support. I assured him I would. As a young man, he had typical struggles but nothing that raised red flags or concerns that he was contemplating ending his life.

The clues that someone is feeling depressed and anxious are often concealed. Connor did not share his feelings and let us know that he was in a dark place. I believe this is for one of two reasons or a combination:

1. He did not want to burden others with his problems. He was the kind of guy who worked things out on his own. As mentioned earlier, he took responsibility for his life circumstances.
2. He did not recognize that his pain was so bad that he needed help. Sometimes you do not know that you need help. If you think you do not need help, then you do not seek it. But help is really what makes a difference.

I frequently see news of celebrities who take their life — people who seemingly have good lives, are happy, and publicly display their happiness. Despite outward appearances, famous celebrities who die by suicide remind us that you never know what another person is going through and, sometimes, not until it's too late. Being successful does not prevent a person from feeling unfulfilled or unhappy.

When Robin Williams, comedian, and actor, died by suicide it rocked my world. I respected him and loved his acting abilities. I wondered how someone who led others to laugh could be in such a dark state.

Marilyn Monroe had everything a person could want: fame, beauty, and money. However, underneath her bombshell looks Monroe reportedly faced many demons, which ultimately led to her death.

When author Ernest Hemingway died in 1961, the world could not believe why such a successful, powerful man would choose to end his life. Apparently, Hemingway suffered decades of physical and mental exhaustion. This had perhaps simply worn the man down in ways that the public never suspected — and that he could not repair.

These celebrities did not outwardly demonstrate their fear, dark feelings, and deepest emotions. There is a good possibility that your loved one was in a similar situation. They disguised their dark feelings, hid them, and did not share them.

In hindsight, you now probably have a better idea of what was going on in their life. I know I do. I found out that Connor was struggling financially, that he talked frequently about his cousin who had committed suicide, and he planned for his dog, Mac, to be taken care of after he died. Connor spread these conversations around, so they were isolated instances, and no one was aware of the other pieces.

One day Connor's struggles became too great. It was one thing piled on top of another. The mountain became too tall to climb, and the challenge too great to overcome. Even though he had suicidal thoughts and ideation, I believe he did not wake up that morning and plan to kill himself. It was the weight and circumstance of that particular day.

He was familiar with the pain and suffering that we feel as a result of other people's suicide. His cousin took her life nine years earlier. Three of his sisters' friends chose suicide. He was not a stranger to the impact. His intention was not to cause pain for me, his sisters, and his friends. He was worn down, and it was just time. Time to end his misery.

Do I wish I had seen the signs? Do I wish he would have talked to me about his problems? Of course, I do. I am not sure that I could have changed anything though. I only had so much information, and it is critically important that I give myself credit for doing what I did with what I knew at the time. Trying to turn the clock back and change the events will not work.

I remember Connor telling me that he loved me to the stars and back. I responded with my usual "times three." That was the last time we spoke.

You may have been blindsided by your loved one's choice, and I hope this discussion gives you some insight and reassurance. Remember, you cannot go back and change events. You can only move forward.

Complexities of Suicide

I was talking with a friend, and he asked me if suicide grief was harder than other types of loss. I took a moment to answer this question, because I have personally struggled with why I feel different in my grief between Courtney, my nine-month-old daughter who died in a daycare accident, and Connor, my twenty-four-year-old son who took his life.

I concluded that suicide bereavement is not harder, because there is no comparison between cancer, illness, or accidental death. All of it is hard. What I did tell him is that child loss by suicide has its own incredibly unique set of challenges. It is messy, it is complicated, and it is different than other modalities of death.

Here are a few things that contribute to the complexities for those of us who are bereaved by suicide:

- Survivors are left with a need to find answers.
- Survivors, especially parents, want to take responsibility for their child's death.
- Survivors experience high levels of guilt.
- There is social stigma around suicide.
- The loss of someone close by suicide increases the risk of those close to them choosing suicide.
- Unlike other nonviolent deaths, the loss of someone by suicide can lend itself to traumatic stress or posttraumatic stress disorder (PTSD).
- Survivors feel a lack of control.
- Dreams and hopes for the future are lost for the deceased and bereaved.
- Suicide is traumatic to the brain and body of those left in its wake.
- It is difficult to find support for survivors of child loss by suicide.
- Survivors tend to focus on how their loved one died rather than the life they lived.

- Some believe taking one's own life is a sin.
- Some may feel ashamed that their loved one took their life.
- Often, survivors want to hide the fact that it was suicide.
- Survivors may feel angry at the deceased.
- Parents, especially, may feel guilty whenever they find themselves being happy or experiencing joy.
- Others expect the survivor to quickly "get over it."
- Child loss is the elephant in the room — it is an enormous, weighty topic, but no one speaks of it.
- Child loss by suicide is an even larger elephant in the room.

Trauma and Suicide

As I mentioned, suicide is complex, complicated, and messy. In addition to experiencing grief, you may develop a traumatic stress response.

The loss of a loved one by suicide can create trauma — trauma that is so emotionally painful, distressing, and shocking that you can experience temporary or ongoing mental and physical health challenges. The chances of being traumatized increase if you are the person who found your loved one.

Reactions to trauma may surface immediately or days, weeks, months, or years after the event. Your reactions will be unique. Not everyone who is a survivor of suicide loss experiences traumatic stress. However, if you feel that you are undergoing traumatic stress, look at the list below for common responses. You may encounter aspects in each of these areas or only one or two.

Responses to Trauma

Physical:
- Difficulty breathing
- Tiredness and fatigue
- Heart palpitations
- Headaches and/or muscle aches
- Changes in sleep patterns

Mental:
- Avoidance of places that remind you of the suicide
- Feeling abandoned, isolated, or powerless
- Confused, foggy, or slowed thinking
- Difficulty concentrating or making decisions
- Feeling trance-like

Emotional:
- Numbness or mood swings
- Feeling depressed, sad, guilty, angry, frustrated, fearful, or irritable
- Longing to be with the person who has passed
- Apathy
- Feeling troubled or distressed when exposed to traumatic news or events

Spiritual:
- Lack of purpose
- Lowered self-esteem

- Questioning your understanding of the nature of evil and suffering
- Asking yourself questions such as: "Who am I? Where am I going? Do I really matter?"
- Inability to forgive

Nicole's Traumatic Event

Nicole came to me after her son died by suicide. She was the one who found him and, as a result, was experiencing traumatic stress.

She was stuck in the exact moment of finding her son. Before he died, he lived with her and did the usual things a son would do. He ate snacks in his bedroom, borrowed her car, and went to work. They had conversations about the future, what he was going to do after graduating college, and his plans with his girlfriend. They were close.

Nicole was unaware that he was unhappy, depressed, or in a dark place. When she arrived home after work and could not open the garage door to the kitchen, she knew something was wrong. She called her son's cell phone and heard it on the other side of the door. She knew he was there yet wondered why he was not answering. She finally went to the front door. As she stepped into the kitchen, she saw her son's body slumped over, blocking the door to the garage.

That was her horrible traumatic event — finding her son's dead, lifeless body. She saw that image every day. I asked her, is it not bad enough that he died once and now he dies every day? Without hesitation she agreed. She shared with me that repeatedly re-enacting that moment caused her to feel anxious, numb, and withdrawn from her friends. She wanted out. She wanted to stop seeing that image. She wanted to remember her son for more than how he died.

I asked Nicole a few questions to help her think differently:

- Do you want to remember how your son lived?
- You will also die at some point. In the end, would you not agree that it does not really matter how you die?
- Would you feel better if you remembered the good times?

Her response to every question was "Yes"; remembering how her son lived was important to her. After giving some thought about how you die, she agreed — it really does not matter. The fact is, death is death. Focusing on how he died was making her sick. She cried all the time and no longer felt like she had a purpose to live. She longed to think of the years she had with him.

The image that she kept seeing became intrusive. Something would initiate the memory, and she did not have the power to stop it. However, even if she could not stop it from happening, she has the power to determine how long she will linger on that image. She has the capacity to determine how she reacts to it.

I suggested that Nicole have pictures of her son on her phone, on the walls, and on the table showing the good times. Anytime the image of her son at the garage door started to creep into her mind, she could focus on the pictures that were strategically placed around her. These happy, memorable images of her son would replace the negative image. This allowed her to focus on how he lived rather than how he died.

Initially, this was a challenge because the pictures of how he lived brought tears. She found that, over time, they were comforting. Nicole started feeling grateful for the time they were together, for the memories they shared, and that he was such a great young man.

The horrific image recurred less and less often. It rarely rears its ugly head anymore because Nicole focuses on how her son lived rather than how he died.

Your Risk of Suicide as a Suicide Loss Survivor

I want to share what I have learned since working with suicide bereaved parents. I realized that some people are stuck in their grief, unable to move out of their depression, and are living a life of just existing. This made me think about the mental and emotional state I was in prior to Connor's suicide. I was a positive person. I had joy in my life. I had purpose. I was physically and mentally healthy.

I wondered, for those who were stuck, what was their mental state prior to the sudden death of their child? What was their life like? Were they happy? Did they have healthy relationships with family? Were they physically healthy?

I was curious: Why were they stuck now? Had any research been completed on this topic? I found one study published in 2015 in which parents of children who passed away by suicide were found to have significantly higher risk of mental and physical health vulnerability prior to the death of their child. After their loss, the risk increased for depression, anxiety, substance abuse, and marital breakup. The prevalence of depression doubled in the two years after the child's suicide. They also experienced a 60 percent increase in the rate of divorce, cancer, and diabetes.

Stated differently, there is a large probability that if you are struggling with the suicide of your child any pre-existing mental health challenges may make it more difficult to process your child loss and move through your grief to healing.

This makes so much sense to me. If you are already struggling with a mental or physical health issue, adding a traumatic death of a child by their own hand makes the process of moving forward significantly more challenging. If you see yourself in this description, then it is important to address your health challenges prior to being able to heal from your loss.

I bring this up because I am not a clinical psychologist, however, I am a mother who has survived the suicide of my son. I am fortunate that I was in a good place with my mental and physical health prior to his death.

Now you might be asking, so what happens to those who are not depressed but also not living your best, joy-filled life and want to find happiness? I encourage you to consider how you will become a suicide loss survivor. As you read this book and learn about the Three Phases to Move through Grief to Healing, you will gain insights and learn tools to cross that rope bridge and rediscover a life of joy and happiness.

Blame and Suicide

Have you been blamed for your loved one's suicide? Your heart is shattered and now this! How could someone even think such a horrible thing? Unfortunately, this happens more often than you realize, with friends and family judging and irrationally placing blame. Accept that you cannot stop them from being negative. This does not suggest they are right. It does mean you can protect yourself and set boundaries.

As the dagger of their negative comment can slice deep into your heart, you may be inclined to have a comeback — a comeback that is as hurtful to them as their comment was to you. You may want to see their pain and anguish. However, spending the time and emotional energy crafting a comeback is a disservice to both of you. Instead, build up boundaries to protect yourself. Do not let others inflict pain and suffering, especially now as you grieve.

Be selective about what you give your time and attention to. Just think, if you put the energy into your grief healing that you put into defending yourself against the negative, how much better off would you be? Possibly you could be accepting your loss, learning to live with it, and rebuilding your life.

When you are offended by someone's blame or negative comment, every other offense is magnified. Have you felt like everything has gone wrong since your loved one's suicide? Is everyone against you? Letting one negative comment in opens a tiny crack in the dam and could allow more negative comments to enter. Eventually the dam breaks and all the blame, worry, and fears come crashing down on you like a tidal wave. Do not let one hurtful and damaging comment get through. Stop accepting the blame — now. Again, protect yourself and set boundaries.

Cocoon Story

Allow me to share a story: Your grief is like a cocoon. In the darkness that surrounds you, you do not know how to get out. One day a small glimmer of hope appears. Then it disappears, and your emotions overwhelm you. Every day you go through the motions of eating, sleeping, and dealing with your grief. Then you see another glimmer of light. This time, it is bigger than the last. It is big enough that you are drawn to it. The motions you are going through become less robotic, and you have more control. Then it hits you again. Grief sets you back, but you remember the light and seek it out.

Now, the beam is now stronger than before. Every day you walk toward that light. You are struggling to work through the pain, frustration, and anger of losing your loved one. It is painful. You hate that this happened. You do not want to feel any more pain.

One day you realize you must face the pain and fear. Each time you do, the light becomes stronger and more encouraging. You now have something to reach for. It has become clear that you must break through the cocoon that has you trapped. Doing so will help you move through your grief to hope — the hope of surviving the suicide loss of your loved one.

One day, you look at yourself in the mirror and realize that if you had not experienced your pain, you would not have focused on the light. The restricting cocoon is what prepared you for what lay ahead, to become a stronger, more resilient person. The light would have been forever hidden. It may not have been your choice to be put into the cocoon, however, you have the choice to break free of it.

You emerge from the darkness transformed. A new and different person. You are now a beautiful butterfly.

Life can present huge obstacles, and you can overcome this obstacle. You would not be as strong as you are today without this experience.

The following chapters guide you, step by step, through the Three Phases to Move through Grief to Healing. As noted earlier, I encourage you to be open to the suggestions, take notes, use the tools that work for you, and be an active participant in your healing process.

CHAPTER 5

PHASE I: ACCEPTANCE

You may be familiar with the five stages of grief developed by Elisabeth Kubler-Ross. Within those five stages, acceptance is the last stage she presents. Why are we starting with acceptance as the first phase in the Three Phases to Move through Grief to Healing? First things first, Kubler-Ross denounced the five stages of grief before she died. She never intended them to be concrete steps or a linear process for grieving.

Second, I developed the Three Phases based on my personal experience. When grappling with the loss of my son, I knew I had to start with acceptance. Plus, I believe the other stages Kubler-Ross mentions — denial, anger, bargaining, and depression — are actually symptoms of grief. We will look at these within the framework of the Three Phases process, addressed throughout the following chapters.

I love a quote from Oprah Winfrey about acceptance. To paraphrase, she noted that "radical acceptance" applies to every challenge in your life. She says that stress comes from wanting something to be different from what it actually is. Once you accept a situation for what it is, then you can make a decision regarding what to do next.

Radical acceptance. I do like the principle. It makes sense in your ever-changing world. Accept what has happened. It is an important step in making a choice with what you have been handed. Choose to process your grief. Live in the moment, and do not try to re-create what cannot be re-created. You have a choice to love life now. You have a new norm. You may be in a dark and heart-wrenching place. You never asked to be in this place, part of this grieving parents' club. I get it. It is difficult.

Acceptance of your loved one's death does not mean that you are forgetting them. You are giving yourself permission to understand they are no longer with you. Death of a loved one will change you. You cannot change this fact. You cannot turn back the clock and take back what has happened. How you deal with the grieving process will determine your ability to move forward.

Acceptance of death does not mean you are left unscathed. Acceptance does not mean that you are healed. It does not mean you are whole again or that your grief is gone. Acceptance and grief are ongoing; they are a process and a journey.

The real problem is that most people in the midst of their sorrow cannot imagine accepting the loss of their loved one. To do so, they feel, would inadvertently mean that the person was not meaningful to them or that they are not worth the pain and sorrow.

To accept is to understand your life has been forever changed because of the loss of your loved one. You will never return to who you were before the loss, yet you will learn to live without your loved one's presence. Out of this, you morph into a new person — just like exiting from that dark cocoon. It is essential to be open to the change. While it may be difficult to see this now, especially in the beginning of your grieving process, it is possible to make something good happen out of tragedy.

The best way to move through grief is to take it as it comes. Expectations of linear progress or completely conquering grief forever are largely unattainable when someone important to you is gone.

The grieving process is not easy. It is not a smooth path. More often than not it is bumpy, uncomfortable, and a rollercoaster ride. One moment you may be happy and suddenly, without warning, you are sad and emotional.

Think of this as a season in your life. It is temporary, and you will pass through it, although the extreme sadness and loss you are currently experiencing feels like it will never lift. You may question if you will ever experience peace, joy, and happiness again.

You can, and you will — if you allow yourself to move forward, one step in front of the other. It is always better to deal with the emotions and feelings as they naturally come through the processing of grief.

Accepting the death of your loved one might be something you feel you will never be able to do. There is something about the finality of their death: you will never hear their voice again, smell their fragrance, feel the intensity of their hug, or see the reassurance of their smile.

If only you had known what the future would hold — you would have held their embrace longer, said those three beautiful words,

"I love you," one more time, or made amends for harsh words or a broken relationship.

I understand each one of those thoughts and have felt the same emotions. However, there comes a point where holding on to these thoughts does not serve you. As difficult as it is, accepting the death of a loved one is quite freeing.

Allow me to set something straight. Acceptance does not mean forgetting their existence, your love for them, or your relationship.

Not accepting their death will keep you in the past while the rest of the world keeps going. As you grieve, have you felt like the world should stop and grieve with you? Although you may wish this could happen, it will not happen. The world is living in the present moment and focused on the future.

Eileen's Acceptance

Not being able to accept her son's death became a stumbling block for Eileen. I say stumbling block, because she was able to work her way over it.

As we talked through the issue of acceptance, I saw how deeply she loves her son, how much she misses him, and how much she misses his daily phone calls. I suggested she write a letter to her son with all these points included. It was important that she express her emotions. In this letter she needed to feel all of them: anger, denial, disappointment, sadness, heartache, and any other emotions that surfaced. As we wrapped up our Zoom session, she promised herself that she would do this even though she feared it would be an extremely painful experience. Eileen doubted me when I told her it would be good, and that with acceptance comes healing.

When we met the following week, she was eager to share about the process of writing her son a letter. She set aside an hour in a quiet, comfortable place to write to her son Tim and was quite surprised how quickly the time flew by. She was able to tell Tim all the things she wanted. Even with the fear of being overcome with crying and sadness, she wrote a love letter to her son. Indeed, she cried, tears dropping on her pages, nose running, and eyes blurry and swollen. Eileen told Tim everything she had been thinking and wanting to tell him since he had been gone.

Writing her letter was her final kiss, hug, and "I love you." Eileen realized that it was time to let go of the expectation that Tim would somehow respond. It was time to accept the reality that he was gone.

Eileen was surprised by how light she felt after finishing her letter. She no longer felt the burden to deny his absence. The light bulb of reality was encouraging. She felt equipped to focus on the present instead of being tied to the past. Even more remarkable, she felt Tim was telling her that she needed to accept he was gone. In her heart she realized she would be okay and that she just climbed over an important stumbling block in her grief journey.

One memory that brought a smile to her was how Tim introduced her to singing karaoke. It was something they had done together at home. Since his death she had not turned on the speakers or picked up the microphone, even to dust it. It had been their special time together. While she missed singing karaoke with him, she was inspired by this memory and grateful for their time together. She decided it was time to sing karaoke again in her son's honor.

Avoidance

If you are not accepting your loss, you could be avoiding your grief. I would like to offer a definition, so you can better understand what you could be experiencing. Avoidance is broadly defined as "To keep away from or stop oneself from doing (something)."

Avoidance is important for grievers to understand. This is a type of coping mechanism that will likely impact your healing from the death of a loved one. Avoidance is not doing something coupled with the pain or fear associated with doing that thing — the thing you need to do. This is called *experiential avoidance*. You desire to prevent unpleasant, difficult thoughts, emotions, and feelings. Your perception of the weight of these feelings impacts your ability to process your grief, loss of control, embarrassment, guilt, shame, or lack of purpose.

Experiential avoidance can lead to long-term consequences. Losing a loved one and not accepting that loss impacts all areas of your life from relationships, your career, your finances, your outlook, your dreams for the future, and your health.

Examples of avoidance in grief include not talking about your loved one, not wanting to be around others, and not participating in activities of living such as showering, eating, and getting dressed.

Are You Avoiding Your Grief?

Again, if you are not accepting your loss, you could be avoiding your grief. Why would you not want to talk about your loved one? You might think the pain is too great and every time you think of them, you might get emotional, angry, or upset. You might avoid going to the grocery store for the fear of crying in public and are embarrassed to let others see you this way.

Avoidance is part of human nature, and you could be all too familiar with the concept. A hallmark of avoidant coping is when you put more effort and thought into how to avoid the activity than finding ways to confront it. Avoidant coping can take on many forms, but the consistent pattern is this: Stressful trigger → negative thought and physical response → feeling overwhelmed → avoiding the activity or thoughts that involve the trigger.

No one wants to miss a loved one. You pursue happiness, the good life, and joy while avoiding sadness, heartache, and pain. Until someone you love dies. They might die unexpectedly, at a young age, by illness, or by their own hand. That does not matter. What does matter is you are now forced to confront some new emotions.

Not knowing how to handle the feelings, you may choose to actively avoid experiencing them. You may not understand that grief and sadness are normal emotions. The onset of a grief wave is sometimes predictable but often not, with each new wave bringing with it an ocean of unpleasant thoughts, reminders, sensations, and memories. Stepping back into life, job, and family responsibilities can limit your ability to grieve. You may have found it necessary to avoid triggers just to get through the day.

A few examples:

- "I avoid going to church, because I fear people will ask me questions, and I am not ready to answer them. I am afraid I will start crying."
- "I avoid the office building where my son died, because every time I go by it triggers memories that hurt."
- "I avoid the hospital, because that is where I last saw my sister alive. I get knots in my stomach."

- "I avoid feeling my grief, because I have been told to get over it."
- "I avoid going to sleep at night, because I think about my son all night."
- "I avoid cleaning the fingerprints off the mirror, because I do not want to forget my daughter."
- "I avoid looking at pictures, because I get angry for lost dreams."

The opposite end of the spectrum is those who can only think of their grief 24/7. Their thoughts are constantly overtaken by the difficult emotions of loss. Does this sound familiar? You might welcome some relief from your grief instead of struggling in it.

Somewhere between avoidance and struggle there is a place that allows you to sit with your grief without being completely swept away by it.

Taking breaks from your grief is healthy through the use of a healthy distraction. The goal of a healthy distraction is to reduce the intensity of unpleasant emotions, so you can more effectively manage them and develop creative solutions to the things that are troubling you.

In this case, taking a break is a form of avoidance, which can be useful for a short time especially when you are dealing with something as painful and enduring as grief. For example, during the first few days after a death, feelings of grief can be overwhelming, yet culture and society dictate that mourners must get dressed, plan services, tie up loose ends, and deal with family and friends. I have often heard people say that they put off crying during those first few days or could not cry even if they tried. The tidal wave of emotions was scary, and they did not want to deal with it at that time and in that environment.

While taking a brief break from your grief can be healthy, it is important to steer clear of the wide variety of unhealthy choices to avoid your emotions and your grief. Remember, avoiding your grief will keep you from accepting your loss. Take a look at a few ways you could be avoiding your grief. When reading the following paragraphs, ask yourself if you are experiencing any of these avoidance techniques.

Drugs and Alcohol as Avoidance

Drugs and/or alcohol are unhealthy coping mechanisms that help you think you are handling your loss. In fact, they are contributing to your denial and avoidance of the circumstances. It is possible, prior to your loss, that you already faced a challenge. Loss of a loved one can add to the complexity of your addiction, or it may even open the doors, pushing you into drug and alcohol use. You must address this area of recovery in addition to healing your grief. There are many treatment options available from in-patient treatment centers to Alcoholic Anonymous, Cocaine Anonymous, and Narcotics Anonymous.

Work/Busyness as Avoidance

Work/busyness is an opportunity to allow your brain not to think about your loss, thus keeping you from accepting it and being able to move forward. In small portions, this can be healthy. You may be surrounded with others who support you and help you to feel productive. Work can also be a place of comfort. The familiarity of the environment and routine is also a way to experience structure, and your thoughts might not be interrupted by the loss that occurred outside of the job. However, to work or be so busy that you neglect to take care of yourself in order to totally ignore the pain is not a positive way to walk through your grief journey.

Caring for Others as Avoidance

Caring for others is a great way to take the focus off your own problems. It is entirely possible to put aside your needs in order to care for others. Boundaries no longer exist, because you have built an internal expectation that you are the only one capable of caring. This can be another type of avoiding your own grief.

Avoidance also can take on the face of "everything is okay." Your grief never surfaces, it seems as though your loss never happened, and you do not share any emotions typically associated with grief.

These are a few examples of how you could be avoiding facing — and accepting — your loss and avoiding your grief. There is one problem with avoiding grief, it is patient. There is nothing in our lives more patient than grief, and it will sit and wait. It will never just go away without being acknowledged and processed. In turn, the pain you do not process will transmit itself outwardly or "sideways." Without even realizing it, you could be damaging your relationships, your health, and your future by not accepting your loss.

Do you think your pain and fears will automatically go away without facing them? Do you recall as a young child having monsters under your bed? One of your parents would come into your room and chase them out — they would face them and take away your fear.

Grief is much the same. It needs to be faced, accepted.

When it is not, your world can shrink as your role as a griever changes with emotions and thoughts impacting who you are. You may no longer make dinner, care for your other children, or conduct self-care.

Brigette's Story — Avoiding Grief with Busyness and Caring for Others

I have known Brigette for over ten years. We started as business partners and friends. She is into healthy eating, and I am into personal training. We had a common bond of health and wellness.

Brigette has a heart of gold and is always doing one more thing for somebody else. However, she is always busy doing things for others, to her own detriment. My friend is like the Energizer Bunny who keeps on giving even when she is in a difficult season.

When we met she was a widow, not just once but twice. She inherited a farm from her first husband that is across the country from where she currently lives. It requires her to travel back and forth to tend to different aspects of the farm's business.

One of her farm hands worked for the family for many, many years. He was more like a member of the family than an employee. When he got to the point that he could no longer work, Brigette tended to his needs. Upon his death, Brigette gave herself no time to grieve. She immediately stepped up to keep the farm going. Meanwhile she was still keeping her own business afloat from afar. She just pushed forward.

Soon thereafter Brigette's sister, Tammy, died. After Tammy's sudden death from a heart attack Brigette made a point to guarantee that Tammy's husband would be cared for. Brigette returned home after several weeks of putting things in order for her brother-in-law and resumed her business activities without skipping a heartbeat, helping him from afar while still tending to the farm's business and managing the apartments she owned.

Recently Brigette experienced the death of another longstanding friend, James. She was with him through cancer treatment, poor health, dementia, and ultimately his death. She was tireless and relentless in making sure he received the care he needed. She spent hours on the phone and working with attorneys, sometimes failing to eat or take care of her own personal needs. Brigette is small yet mighty.

I learned of James's death via Facebook when Brigette posted of his passing. I called her to express my condolences, talk about her friend, and more importantly to check in with her. As with all the previous deaths, it was apparent that she quickly became consumed with busyness, which took her away from feeling her grief. She gave herself very little time to process her losses. She did not stop.

We decided to meet for dinner, and, after our usual hugs, we settled in for our heart-to-heart conversation. I pointed out that she was not giving herself the time and space to accept her losses and give herself permission to grieve. Brigette agreed wholeheartedly. I noticed she looked more frazzled than usual.

As we chatted, she explained that she did not have time to slow down. There were too many things to do and so many people counting on her. I agreed but questioned whether this could be detrimental for her mental and physical health. She also shared she was not getting adequate sleep. The long hours she was putting in day after day were not allowing her to feel — anything. Through her busyness she was avoiding her pain and suffering. This is her standard way of dealing with grief.

While we caught up on what was going on in each other's lives, I could tell that her mind was racing with everything on her to-do list. I felt she wanted to talk, so I offered to listen to stories of James, Tammy, and others. She shared beautiful memories of her sister and her friend with a few tears sliding down her cheek. As the evening progressed, without an agenda, Brigette relaxed and slowed down. This evening of non-busyness was just what she needed. She was finally giving herself time to grieve. She knew I understood, as I too have walked this grief journey multiple times.

It was evident that a huge weight was lifted from her tiny frame. In the few hours we were together, Brigette did more grief work than she had in months, maybe even years. She admitted it felt good to step away from the demands of others. She was able to remove the noise and clutter of the outside world and focus inward.

Brigette recognized that her busyness was getting in the way of her healing. From now on, she was not going to let that happen. Right then and there, she put time in her calendar to "unplug" for a few hours every week. Checking back with her a month later, she told me the dedicated time to herself was working. She was accepting her losses and feeling her pain, which was healing and allowing her to move forward in her grief.

If You Are Not Accepting Your Loss, You Could be Avoiding Your Grief

It takes intentional healing to walk your grief journey. Leaving it to happenstance does not work. Sometime later, not sure when, your unresolved grief will come back with full fury. For many it can become a harmful cycle that persists to the detriment of personal healing.

Avoiding seemingly painful stimuli might prove beneficial in the immediate, but it is a short-term solution. It is like taking an aspirin to treat a broken arm; it may temporarily dull the pain. If you choose not to address the broken bone, you will never be able to heal. In order to gain understanding, perspective, and tolerance for the pain of grief, you need to allow yourself to actually feel it — face it — in the present moment and in the future.

Confronting grief as it comes, expressing yourself, experiencing pain, and seeking help are the best strategies for true healing. However, if over time your signs and symptoms are not letting up, seriously consider reaching out to someone for help.

Being stuck in grief is hard on your health: physical, mental, emotional, and spiritual. When you continue to grieve over a child who passed, you take away the opportunity to continue the bond you had with them. When you are sad, it gets in the way of having positive thoughts of them or joyful memories. You owe it to yourself and to the memory of your loved one to give yourself the best possible chance to move through grief to healing in a healthy way.

You are here, reading this book to move through grief to healing. It is my utmost goal and prayer that you sidestep the hurdles of avoidance. The best way to move through your grief is by embracing it, when and where it happens. Accept that the grieving process is not linear and accept that it is a journey, which sometimes circles back around giving you pangs of pain.

You owe it to yourself and the person who passed to give yourself the best possible chance to move forward in a healthy and positive way. The first step to do so is acceptance. The next three chapters delve deeper into the topic of acceptance with a focus on understanding your grief, giving yourself permission to grieve, and giving yourself permission to heal.

CHAPTER 6

PART 1: UNDERSTAND YOUR GRIEF

When you understand that life and death are part of the circle of life you will gain clarity about your grief and the grieving process. As a philosophical concept, the circle of life means you start at the end and end at the beginning. Your life, from start to finish, resembles a complete 360-degree circle. No matter how big or how small, it ends for all of us. Death is guaranteed to happen for each of us.

Death and loss are part of our circle of life and a painful reality. Everyone reacts to it uniquely, and the effects may remain for months or years. It is your response to your loss that impacts your ability to live a fulfilling and productive life. You have a choice.

As a reminder, we are stepping through the Three Phases to Move through Grief to Healing. In this chapter, we will continue our discussion of acceptance and, specifically, we will discuss the need to understand your grief. To refresh your memory, Phase I — Acceptance has three parts:

- Part 1: Acceptance — Understand Your Grief
- Part 2: Acceptance — Permission to Grieve
- Part 3: Acceptance — Permission to Heal

Child Loss

As a mother you possibly have the expectation that your child should outlive you. To some people, a child who dies before a parent is a violation of the natural order of things. This is called out-of-order death. While it may seem that way, there is no guarantee that children outlive their parents. There is nothing that indicates the guaranteed chronological order of death. For millennia it was common for parents to experience the death of a child.

The perceived premature passing of a child dashes dreams and hopes for the future. With it are gone birthday celebrations, graduations, weddings, and grandchildren. It is said that losing a child is the worst pain imaginable. It is a horrible heart-wrenching experience. However, given that death is part of the circle of life, you can emerge from the loss and learn to live without your loved one, still retain fond memories of your child, and go on to live a fulfilling, productive life.

This concept of living a productive life applies to you — it enables you to move forward after loss. I encourage you to continue on this journey, do not let the past hold you back, and allow yourself to live for the present moment and embrace the future.

Now that you understand life and death as it relates to the circle of life, let's take a closer look at grief, so you can gain a deeper understanding of your grief.

What Is Grief?

Grief is the internal thoughts and feelings you have when a loved one dies. It is a strong feeling of sadness. It is natural to experience grief. It is normal to miss a loved one.

Grief has many faces. It is individual, and your grief is no better or worse than another's. This is not a place or time to compare pain and suffering. It is a journey. Emotions associated with grief are difficult to understand.

The intensity of your grief is linked with the depth of love between you and your deceased child. As a human you are meant to experience pain and suffering. There is no guarantee that life will be easy. It is expected to experience challenges.

Find solace in the fact that the human experience naturally includes loss and pain. It is a universal experience. No matter what your unique experience, you can move through grief to healing. There is hope.

Acute Symptoms of Grief

Shortly after a loss is experienced, you can enter into acute phases of grief. Acute grief is characterized by changes in physical, mental, emotional, and spiritual health. Symptoms of acute *physical* grief can include:

- Trouble initiating or maintaining sleep
- Chest heaviness or pain
- Shortness of breath

- Lack of desire to eat
- Headache
- Digestive issues
- Broken heart syndrome (discussed below)

Symptoms of acute *mental* grief can include:

- Forgetfulness
- Difficulty concentrating
- Slowed thinking
- Wandering aimlessly
- Feeling trance-like
- Prevailing need to retell the story of your loved one's death

Symptoms of acute *emotional* grief can include:

- Fear
- Guilt
- Longing to be with the person who has passed
- Loneliness
- Apathy
- Anger

Symptoms of acute *spiritual* grief can include:

- Lack of purpose
- Lowered self-esteem
- Withdrawn and isolated

- Negativity
- Inability to forgive

Broken Heart Syndrome

There is one physical symptom I want to dive into deeper. Broken heart syndrome deserves some special attention on its own. Broken heart syndrome was first recognized in Japan in 1991 by the Japanese cardiovascular specialist known simply as Sato. Broken heart syndrome is also known as takotsubo cardiomyopathy or stress cardiomyopathy.

What is broken heart syndrome? The general hypothesis is that when you experience the loss of a loved one or extreme grief the release of stress hormones can trigger cardiac abnormalities that adversely affect the heart muscle, which should be taken seriously.

Common symptoms are chest pain, fainting, weakness, low blood pressure, irregular heartbeat, shortness of breath, sweating, nausea, weakness in the heart, and heart failure. If you are experiencing symptoms of this condition, please consult your doctor.

While this is a dangerous condition, it is treatable. You may need to seek medical care. I also know that taking care of yourself and working on your physical, mental, emotional, and spiritual health will help you to overcome this challenge.

Remember, there are many physical, mental, emotional, and spiritual symptoms from grief including broken heart syndrome. The symptoms I mentioned above are only a sample of what you could be experiencing.

Learning the Different Types of Grief
Helps You Understand Your Grief

You may be surprised to learn that there are many different types of grief. Understanding which type of grief you are experiencing will help your healing process. In the descriptions that follow, look for yourself. You may have characteristics of several types of grief and possibly cycle in and out of them. Identify the top three types of grief that are the strongest for you.

Normal Grief

Your circumstances are unique and personal. Normal grief, also known as uncomplicated grief, is defined by the American Psychological Association as grief that lasts six months to two years following the loss of someone extremely close to you (either in death or a severed relationship).

While there is a time period applied to normal grief, it is important to know that the definition of normal grief changes in various cultures and over time. Do not feel pressured by the current American attitude to return to normal within weeks, if not days. In a study conducted by WebMD in 2019, it was determined that more than half of Americans are grieving the loss of someone close to them during the last three years. Few Americans feel that the grief period ends at the three-year mark. This is a valid reason to learn coping skills and have the confidence to handle your current and future losses.

Anticipatory Grief

Anticipatory grief is feeling the loss prior to someone's passing. This usually occurs in cases of terminal diseases such as cancer. The dying process is prolonged with fear and anxiety being high. For instance, during the COVID-19 pandemic you might have experienced anticipatory grief due to the unknown: Will you lose a loved one?

Anticipatory grief can be as intense as other forms of grief and include both mental and physical issues that can disrupt your normal life and schedule.

It is important to know that anticipatory grief is normal, especially when it is tied to a close family member or friend who will soon pass away. This is your body and brain's way of recognizing and preparing for the inevitable.

Absent Grief

Absent grief is defined as a lack of grief in the aftermath of a death or the loss of an important relationship. Absent grief can be found in the aftermath of anticipatory grief. The grieving has been done prior to death. The loved one's death may even bring relief, especially for someone who was in pain, sick, and suffering.

Delayed Grief

Delayed grief is suppressed grief until it is triggered by another form of loss such as divorce, job, and so forth. It is just as it sounds — a delayed onset of grief following the severing of a connection with someone else.

For instance, delayed grief can be caused by growing up in a culture or environment that discourages grieving. Or it can be due to feeling as though you should not grieve for this person and masking those emotions, even from yourself. Or it can simply be caused by not wanting to face the situation and applying some of the avoidance techniques mentioned in the previous chapter. Your brain plays tricks on you until something happens that makes the loss a reality.

Complicated Grief

Complicated grief is the inability to accept a loved one's passing. Typically, if you are experiencing complicated grief, you shut yourself off from friends or family and lose additional relationships, making it difficult to recover due to isolation, loneliness, and paralysis. Complicated grief is also known as traumatic or prolonged grief, and it is a diagnosis you can receive from a medical doctor.

Prolonged Grief

Prolonged grief impacts normal functioning and can be responsible for medical and mental health issues. The loss traveler frequently ties their self-worth and identity to the one who has passed. You lose all desire to move through your loss.

Prolonged grief can act and feel like depression. With prolonged grief it is difficult to adapt to the change from loss. You may feel a loss of identity and normalcy — a loss of sense and self-worth. To move forward is to feel you are betraying the person who is deceased, possibly due to a codependent relationship.

Codependency is forming your sense of self and worth from someone else instead of developing it from within. If you are in a codependent relationship, you take on the responsibility of making the other person happy, and you do not know who you are without them. For example, you identify as the mother of your child instead of as an individual person with many roles and different types of relationships such as spouse, parent, friend, business professional, and community volunteer.

Disenfranchised Grief

Disenfranchised grief is when there is a lack of societal support such as the loss of a pet. It can also apply to those who grieve over the death of favorite celebrities. To grieve over a pet or a celebrity may be passed off as trivial and you receive little to no understanding. Society denies your right to grieve because it is not a loss of human life.

Chronic Grief

Chronic grief is when the severity of grief does not reduce over time. It is at the same level years later as when the loss first occurred. Chronic grief has been considered by some doctors as a way for those grieving to hold on to a loved one by upholding their memory or promises made.

Distorted Grief

Distorted grief is being angry at the world with the possibility of doing harm to others or yourself. In the case of losing your loved one to suicide, you may be fantasizing about joining your loved one by taking your own life. If this is you, seek help immediately! The risk of hostility, fighting, and self-harm increases with distorted grief. You may blame others for the passing of your loved one. It is normal to experience anger but not for a prolonged period of time.

Cumulative Grief

Cumulative grief is when one loss is added on top of another. You may feel as though you are doing well but then another loss is piled on, and you do not know how to handle it. This is especially hard when the time between losses is extremely short. You do not have time to process one loss before the other occurs.

When losses are spread out, most generally, you have time to process and heal. If you are experiencing cumulative grief, seek help to walk through each and every loss. Please do not do it alone. During the COVID-19 pandemic, for instance, many people experienced cumulative grief as the pandemic added to already existing grievances such as a family member being in hospice or a job loss, while regularly hearing of extended family, friends, and acquaintances who perished from COVID-19.

Exaggerated Grief

Exaggerated grief is magnified grief through actions and words. It can ultimately cause serious mental health issues. It can lead to major psychiatric disorders such as phobias as a result of hyper-grieving thoughts, actions, and words.

Masked Grief

Masked grief is when a person denies there is any loss, therefore, there is no reason to grieve. Men commonly demonstrate this type of grief more than women. Modern-day culture dictates that men must be tough, unemotional, and strong.

It is dangerous to mask grief. All emotions are rejected — and not accepted — which does not give you the proper time and space to heal. Remember, grief is normal. And necessary.

Traumatic Grief

Traumatic grief is when the loss occurs suddenly and usually violently. In other words, tragedy is at the heart of it. You are traumatized by the loss, which may spark fear, anxiety, nightmares, and more. Traumatic grief is often experienced by those left behind after terrorist attacks, deadly car crashes, drownings, suicide, and more.

Collective Grief

Collective grief is the type of grieving experienced by communities or societies. It is most often talked about in regard to a major celebrity's death.

For many in the United States, there is a massive collective grief that is ongoing due to multiple traumatic and unnerving events that have been highly publicized. Examples include gun shootings in schools, shopping malls, and other public places. On a worldwide scale, you may have experienced collective grief around the COVID-19 pandemic.

Inhibited Grief

Inhibited grief is when someone shows some signs of grieving but not nearly to the level or intensity based on the relationship that has been severed. Remember, grief and its intensity is usually related to the depth of love and closeness of the relationship with the deceased.

Abbreviated Grief

Abbreviated grief is a short-lived grief in which the person who is grieving feels that they should move on quickly. Or they possibly feel they have experienced their grief and are healed. Be aware though, the grief may resurface at any time. You see this with folks who remarry quickly after the death of a partner. Abbreviated grief does not mean that the person is not still grieving.

As you learn more about your grief, it will help to facilitate your progress. There is no right or wrong type of grief. It is important to accept it for what it is, then move forward to make progress in your healing.

Grief is not new to life, but you may have questions about grief and the grieving process. Please see Appendix 2 for a comprehensive list of commonly asked questions about grief with my answers.

Now that you have a better understanding of grief, allow me to help you to start actively moving through your grief and the first stage of acceptance: Understand your grief.

Journaling as a Tool to Understand Your Grief

Journaling is the tool I return to in times of stress, discomfort, and pain. Trust this simple tool. It will help. Journaling can play an important role in your healing. Why journal? To be honest, it is the easiest of all things to do. It is accessible to everyone. All you need is a pencil or pen and paper. It can be taken anywhere and done anytime. There is no right or wrong way to journal.

While going through the loss of my first daughter, I know that my friends found it difficult to understand my grief and heartache. I learned it was tough to talk to them, to convey how I felt. Writing down my thoughts in whatever way they spilled out of my head helped me to feel like somebody utterly understood, even if that somebody was a pad of paper. The paper did not judge.

The journal is a safe place to express my thoughts. It is my best friend, because it holds my secrets, my fears, my anger, and my heartache.

Seeing my thoughts on paper allowed me to view them differently. Sometimes, seeing my troubles in writing lessened the severity. It allowed me to have hope that things would get better.

There were many times I cried as I wrote. Tears often stained the page and blurred the ink. It did not matter how the page looked. My thoughts were out of my head. Writing down my thoughts often left me exhausted while at the same time helping me to heal.

What Kind of Journal?

Buy a notebook that will be special to you. You may want a simple school composition notebook or one that is colorful, possibly with a design that makes you feel good. You can get the wide-ruled or college lines or use a blank notebook. Choose whatever is right for you.

Grab several pens because you want to make sure they work. When your thoughts are flowing freely, you do not want to run out of ink and go searching for another pen. You may find different color inks also help. If you are feeling a particular emotion, you may want to use a certain color.

If you are concerned about keeping your journal safe, there are a couple of options to ensure that it is for your eyes only. You can purchase a file box that has a lock and key and keep it in there. You can also purchase a journal that has a lock on it. A journal retains your deepest, innermost thoughts, so make sure it is in a secure place.

How to Journal

When you sit down to write, find a place that is safe to express your emotions. They will come out on paper and come out physically.

I highly suggest journaling at the same time daily. I prefer to write every morning before I get out of bed. Well, almost. I grab a cup of tea and then crawl back into bed to write. My notebook and pens sit on my nightstand, so I know where they are.

Journal when the time is right for you. If you want to jot down your thoughts while they are fresh, carry your journal with you. Journaling before going to bed may be the right time for you to let go of the day's events. Multiple daily entries may be what you need. Whenever or how many times you journal is up to you.

Journaling is a free flow of your thoughts. There is no judgment, right or wrong, punctuation, or time limit. Feel free to cuss. Open your heart and let the pen flow. The only thing I recommend is to start each entry by dating it. Add the time if you are writing several times during the day. This will be helpful later.

After that, it is all about how you feel. If you are angry, write it down. Include why you are angry. It seems obvious you would be angry because your loved one is gone. Yes, that is the truth, but as you grieve, you can lash out to others in anger. Maybe someone cut you off in traffic, maybe someone was rude to you, maybe your spouse does not understand why you stayed in your pajamas all day.

You may be feeling guilty for what happened. The guilt as a parent, repeatedly asking why this happened, is one of the worst feelings. Write it down.

You may be sad. What triggered your sadness? Write it down. By getting it down on paper, you can process your thoughts and emotions and see that you are not insane. Get it all out.

You may want to talk to your loved one. As weird as it seems, I often document conversations with loved ones who passed. I tell them I miss them. I also share what happened during the day. Yes, it is a one-sided conversation, yet it allows me to feel connected. Write it down. I believe your loved one hears and sees you. Let them know you still love them and think of them.

Confusion and desperation can seep into your thoughts. You may not know what to do next. Write it down, including any possible solutions or ideas. Seeing things on paper helps with clarity. Seeing your confusing thoughts written down helps to visualize the extent of these issues. You can use this information later to put things in order or decide your next step.

Journaling is also a place to remember your loved one. I think one of the greatest fears is that the recollections will fade away. With that fear, you try to keep all those memories in your head at all times, which is impossible to do. Write down your remembrances, so they are preserved forever. As you write, more times, places, and events will pop into your head. Write these down too and remember the happy times, the times you spent together. Capturing your memories in your journal will enable you to come back to revisit them any time you desire.

Eileen's Story, Continued

It is very exciting when my clients make breakthroughs early in their journey. It truly sets the stage for greater healing and faster recovery. Breakthroughs occur as they grasp the concepts I teach. Eileen, whom I first wrote about in Chapter 5, experienced a big jump in her healing once she understood the effectiveness of journaling.

Eileen was struggling with sleep. At nighttime, when she was done for the day, ready to go to bed, she consistently thought of her son.

She developed a mental checklist that she reviewed nightly and again each morning. She thought of the last time she saw him, their last day together, and their last hug. Also on her checklist was their final phone call, what they chatted about, recalling that he told her he would see her soon, and exchanging those precious words, "I love you."

Eileen ran through this exhaustive list every night as she was going to sleep. Thinking about this made it difficult to go to sleep, and these disturbing thoughts interrupted her sleep. The rest she so desperately desired alluded her.

In the morning, those same thoughts would go through her mind before she even opened her eyes. This set the tone for her day, which was one of sadness with a focus on her loss. She was in a vicious tornado, being bashed about, not knowing how to get out.

I thought journaling would be the perfect tool for this situation. When I asked her if she was willing to follow my suggestion, she answered yes. She longed for a good night's sleep. Lack of sleep was starting to impact her physical health and cause confusion. She lacked the ability to think clearly and was having difficulty focusing.

The next afternoon, Eileen wrote down every detail she could remember, everything she thought of at night and again in the morning. She spent hours writing all she could think of. Where she was at the time, what they had talked about, what they had laughed about. She included everything. The phone call informing her that her son died, who she called to share the news, and what she did next.

The facts had played in her mind like a broken record. She had been afraid that she would forget them, even those she would rather not remember. Every night she had felt obligated to remember every detail.

Once Eileen put it all down on paper, she let go of the need to remember. It was now all safely documented in her journal. The details were in a safe place, preserved forever. She no longer felt obligated to spend mental and physical energy on the process of remembering all the details. She let go and felt released of the great burden.

Eileen discovered she was able to go to sleep easily. Instead of running through her checklist, she started to read again, something she had not done since her son passed. She slept through the night, and the only thing on her mind in the morning was a good cup of coffee. She started to focus on making healthy food choices. This in turn made improvements in her thinking, increased her motivation to exercise, and helped her rebuild relationships.

Journaling empowered Eileen to release consuming thoughts of the past and, instead, focus on the present and look forward to the future. She was filled with the hope of being able to move through her grief to further healing.

Measure Your Progress

Remember when I suggested you date your journal entries? Go back to the beginning and look at them. Looking back at your entries is a measurement of your progress. It is an evaluation of where you are in the journey. The progress is yours to see. Nobody else is measuring this. It is for you only.

How often you look back depends on your desire to see your progress. In the first few weeks, you may not see or feel any progress. At the one-month mark, you may see an ever-so-slight shift in your thinking. I saw a transition at three months. I was coming to terms with my loss and able to look at my future.

There are two paths you may experience. The first is you see that things are getting better. I am not saying that you will ever get over the loss of your child. What I am saying is that you are starting to move through this difficult season in your life. You may notice that you are not as sad every day. There may be fewer tears. You are able to see some happiness in the day. You may see some hope for the future. You may see light. You may want to do more.

By going back and reading my entries, I noticed small increments of progress. Initially, I described my pain and heartache. There were times I could not see through the tears to write. Then I started including what I was grateful for instead of only focusing on the sadness. I found great relief when I started using metaphors in my journaling.

This is one of my favorite metaphors: Something about dead trees grabs my attention with their knots, twisted branches, and displaced roots. There is an artistic beauty in them. God created them. In life they provided shade and shelter from storms and protected the landscape with their lives. When they lost their battle with Mother Nature, they now serve a different purpose. As a damaged, fallen tree they supply shelter for the smallest animals. As they rot, they provide nutrients to fertilize the soil and provide new life and new beginnings.

As I pondered this thought, it came to mind that children's lives were like fallen trees. They had great lives. They impacted and influenced others around them. This comforted me to recognize that in their short lifespan they made a difference. After pondering this new perspective, I found my days were better, even if only slightly. I could laugh. I could smile. The darkness was diminishing. I saw all this through my writing.

You may experience the second path: You see a lack of progress. You may find yourself feeling isolated, crying even more, and thinking that things will never get better. You may even think about ending your life, so you can be with your loved one. You may feel depressed. Grief has many layers, and depression is not a normal part of it. Rather, it is an impediment to moving through grief. If this describes how you feel, please seek help. Sometimes it takes multiple modalities to heal. These can include medication, talk therapy, and what I refer to as "wholistic" healing. It is okay to ask for help. In fact, it may be the critical step in your healing process.

Wow, we covered a lot of ground in this chapter! We learned about grief and the different symptoms of grief associated with your physical, mental, emotional, and spiritual health. We also looked at the different types of grief, so you can better understand the grief you are experiencing. And we discussed journaling as a simple, practical, and effective tool to move through grief to healing. The next two chapters continue to guide you through Phase I — Acceptance with two vital steps in your grief journey: giving yourself permission to grieve and giving yourself permission to heal.

CHAPTER 7

PART 2: PERMISSION TO GRIEVE

When it comes to moving from grief to healing, experiencing emotions simply has no replacement. You cannot heal your emotional trauma without physically showing it. For example, if you hurt your arm playing a sport, you would not ignore the physical pain and not have it evaluated with an x-ray. The x-ray offers insight about your injury, much like emotions telling your body you are grieving.

Experiencing loss is a natural occurrence in life and so are the feelings and emotions that come with it. Giving yourself permission to grieve is normalizing those feelings and will help you to heal easier. Remember to give outward expression to the internal anguish of your soul. Do not hide from those expressions or feel ashamed of them. They are what they are — a natural, normal response.

Grieving is not a weakness. There is strength in being vulnerable. It is normal to cry just as when you are injured, sleep when you are tired, or eat when you are hungry.

Society and culture encourage you to hide your pain and appear as though you've "got it all together." You might even shy away from your own pain, fearing that if you let your feelings have free rein you will be seen as "out of control." Your mind might rebel against the idea of anyone seeing your pain, how deeply affected you are, how not okay you feel inside. But expressing your grief is an important step on the road to healing.

An important loss that has not been grieved is unfinished business. It interferes with your ability to approach the world with the whole of your being, be yourself, and enjoy life again. Instead, you stay in a sort of psychological and emotional limbo where, of course, you logically "know" that your loved one has passed away, but you continue to rail against full acceptance of this fact. You live a sort of half-here/half-there existence where you do not feel complete, where you constantly deal with a sort of low-grade psychic and emotional "fever" that keeps you from fully embracing life with all its opportunities and possibilities.

Pain and Grief

You might worry that you will drown in your grief but refusing to grieve is itself a prolonged drowning. Only by submerging yourself fully in your grief can you make it back to the shore. And you cannot heal what you do not feel.

The stories you tell yourself might be stopping you as well. Maybe you think you should just get over it, or you keep telling yourself that other people are far worse off than you, leaving you with no room or justification for feeling your grief. You might even interpret grieving as letting go. Letting go does not mean releasing memories or forgetting your loved one. It is about allowing yourself to heal and move forward.

Perhaps you do not give yourself permission to grieve, because you are afraid of what might happen if you let down your guard. Grief is a dark, unknown abyss, and the secret fear is that if you allow yourself to sink into it you will never find your way back out. There is fear associated with grieving. I will be going deeper into those fears later in this book.

Expressing your grief is essential on the road to healing. The reality is that when you can realize it is okay to hurt, it is okay to not be strong, it is okay to give outward expression to the inner turmoil then you have opened the door to healing.

Fear of pain is one the biggest reasons people do not grieve. Fear is understandable, yet it is common to forget that loss is universal, and everyone will experience it. In truth, it is abnormal to not step into the process of grief.

You might fear that letting yourself grieve will result in dysfunction, but just the opposite is true. Dysfunction arises from carrying unfinished grief around for months or years or the rest of your life. Maladjustment resulting from unfinished grief can be subtle and sometimes difficult to identify. Slowly it can creep into your relationships, affecting how you see and respond to the world. It affects your sense of self. It affects your ability to derive joy out of your experiences. It affects the projects you undertake or the projects you do not undertake.

During times like this, it is important to be intentional with your healing, be kind and patient with yourself, allowing yourself to go through the grief process.

You Have a Choice

Do you want your grief to control your life, or do you want to be in charge of your life? It takes vulnerability to push through the reasons why you will not allow yourself to grieve. Grief is saying goodbye to how things were and then moving forward with your changed circumstances as they are now.

You might refuse to grieve, because you want to deny your loss and deny that mortality exists. This is like having one foot in acceptance and the other in denial.

Courage to Grieve

Mortality may have you questioning your existence, your purpose, your career, your relationships, and the meaning of life. And when a loved one passes away, especially a child, you are forced to confront your own mortality.

Gaining the courage to grieve can start with the dual realizations that mortality is an unavoidable fact of life whether you want it to be or not — and that your loved one would surely want something better for you than sleepwalking through your life because you are not able to let go of how things were. To make way for how things really are, you have to let go of how they were.

The leap of faith of accepting your circumstances the way they are now allows room for healing on the other side of grief. And there *is* healing after loss. You just have to gain the courage to walk that path.

Others may not understand the depth of your pain. And it is not their job to understand your grief, for it is yours and yours alone. They cannot walk this path for you. You must do it. You will face the challenges and fears and learn to embrace the present.

You Are not Broken

You are not broken — you are grieving. Grief is not a problem to be solved, rather a journey to be traveled. It will take time to move through it. Giving yourself permission to grieve may be the best gift you can give yourself during a time of loss. You do not need permission from other people to grieve.

Remember, grief is a process. Death is part of the circle of life. Ignoring your pain and suffering will not make it go away and will not make it better. In fact, stuffing it can have serious consequences on your health.

CHAPTER 8

PART 3: PERMISSION TO HEAL

W hy do you need permission to heal? Giving yourself permission to heal is another important step in your grief journey. In this chapter, you will learn some simple steps to give yourself permission to heal.

It is an irony that grievers often do not take care of themselves and put themselves last on the healing ladder. They put it off until later, and later may never come. Eventually they experience more complex chronic symptoms of grief. They get to the point that the symptoms cannot be ignored. At this time, the choice is to get help or sink.

As you have read throughout this book, it is of the utmost importance to process your grief. It is possible that you will not follow the process outlined in this book, and you might reach a crisis. If that does happen, run — do not walk — to get the help you need.

Approach your healing as an opportunity to practice self-love. Think of yourself as being deserving of happiness, energy, and joy. Give yourself permission to love yourself enough to take care of yourself.

As someone who has survived the loss of many family members, I encourage you to give yourself permission to heal. As a fellow griever, I understand your challenges. I also know that it is possible to move through those challenges and come out the other side. Do it now. Do it today. Give yourself permission to heal.

"Why Do I Feel Guilty?"

If you are like many mourners, you deny yourself permission to heal, because you might be experiencing guilt. This may be especially true for mothers who lost a child to suicide.

Upon reviewing the events leading up to the death of a loved one, you might consider some of the things you could have done differently. This is when guilt shows its ugly face. Seven types of guilt have been identified in the grieving process. As you read the following list, ask yourself if you are feeling any of these types of guilt.

Seven Types of Guilt

1. *Survivor guilt* — This one can truly keep you awake at night. You feel guilty because you are alive and your loved one is not. Or you think it should have been you who died instead of your loved one. You might even ask "Why them?" You would offer yourself to take their place.

2. ***Benefit guilt*** — Are you the financial beneficiary of someone's death? It is possible to feel guilty for receiving money as the result of a loved one's passing.

3. ***Role-failure guilt*** — You look back on your relationship and feel bad, because you believe you were not a good enough mother. When a person you care about dies, guilt may surface, and you can get stuck in "shoulda": You believe you should have done something differently or better, or you should not have done something in the relationship. It is easy to dwell on all the past wrongs, whether real or imagined.

4. ***Death-causation guilt*** — The perception of being responsible for a loved one's death is the driving force with death-causation guilt. Although you did not directly cause the death, you may feel that you should have or could have done something, *anything*, to prevent the death. Another type of "shoulda": "I should have talked them out of joining the military," or "I should have discouraged them from leaving," or "I should have noticed the warning signs that something was wrong."

5. ***Grief guilt*** — Have you somehow felt that you were not grieving right: crying enough, angry enough, sad enough, tough enough? Keep in mind, there are multiple types of grief. Grief is individual. Remember, you grieve however you grieve. There is absolutely no right or wrong way.

6. ***Recovery guilt*** — Have you laughed again? Done things for pleasure? Gotten involved in new activities? Learned to live life without your loved one? Have you felt guilty about

it? This is one of the most significant challenges in coping with a death. After someone you love dies, you still get out of bed every morning (even though you may not feel like it). Time keeps moving and suddenly it has been a month. You know when it has been exactly a month because that date has been forever etched in your brain. Months turn into years, and you realize that you have no choice but to live your life, even though it is not the one you wanted. Time has forced you to move forward. You realize that moving forward does not mean forgetting. You will never forget the life this wonderful person lived. But time has moved you forward, and guilt may arise.

7. *Unmentionable guilt* — This is guilt associated with information that is too terrible to tell. Was your loved one's death due to alcohol or drug abuse? Was their death at their own hand, by suicide? Was there physical or sexual abuse involved? You might be thinking you should have done more to help them. Remember, you were doing your best with what you knew at the time of your loved one's death. In hindsight, it is easy to get trapped in the "shoulda" mentality. Release yourself of that thought. It serves no purpose for the past or the future.

Other Things that Might Be Holding You Back

As you work to give yourself permission to heal, you may identify other things that are holding you back. You might feel selfish for grieving and healing. Ask yourself, "How would my healing positively impact those around me, my family, my work, and my other relationships?"

If you are feeling bad about the investment in yourself, consider the cost of *not* moving forward. Extended grief can affect your health, your career, and your future. So, by investing in yourself as soon as possible, you can save yourself thousands of dollars down the road, plus you will have the knowledge and tools you need to move forward in your healing.

Take the Time to Work on Yourself

Make a point of setting aside thirty to sixty minutes a day to journal to feel your emotions. Many people find this dedicated time to be especially useful. They know it is time to cry, be angry, and let it all out. They find they look forward to this time. It gives them permission to grieve. And when the time is set aside, they find grief tends to wait until that special moment. It is as if you are training your brain to grieve at a certain time, without judgment or fear.

As you progress through your grief, you will find there are more activities you can add to help you navigate through your grief. This is an exciting time to be open to change and see your progress.

Feel Better by Giving Yourself Permission to Heal

Feel better knowing there are others who have traveled this journey before you. You are not alone. You do not need to recreate the wheel; a process with tools has been created for you.

Feel better knowing you can manage the healing experience. The tools you learn in this book will equip you to deal with your grief.

Feel better knowing you can survive the death of your child. You do not have to deny your loss. You can express your emotions and safely negotiate this path. Open yourself to the possibility that you can have the help you need to move through your loss to healing.

Feel better in understanding your grief. There are things you can do to help yourself.

Feel better knowing it is okay to express your emotions.

Feel better knowing you are giving yourself permission to heal. You are doing the right thing.

Feel better that you are progressing. You may not see it but look back a day, a week, or a month, and you will realize your pain has lessened and you have seen a glimmer of hope and joy.

Give yourself permission to heal, and you can and will move forward. Even with that in mind, healing can be a bumpy and painful journey. However, it is the best path forward. Congratulations! You have taken an important step.

**"Pain is inevitable. Suffering is an option."
—Peggy Green**

Katie's Oxygen Mask

During one of my coaching sessions, Katie told me she felt guilty about taking time to cope with her grief and anxiety with the upcoming holidays. We spent some time talking about why she felt guilty. She revealed that her sister-in-law told her that she should be focusing on her children rather than taking care of her own needs. I shared with her this analogy about the oxygen mask.

I asked her to recall watching the flight attendant demonstrate how to use an oxygen mask in the event the airplane lost cabin pressure. The flight attendant explains that if you are traveling with small children or someone who is elderly or handicapped, you must put on your oxygen mask first. You are expected to do this, so you can help those around you. If you pass out because you did not help yourself first, then you cannot help someone else.

When Katie realized that coping tools were like the oxygen mask, she no longer felt guilty for the time she was taking to learn and practice them. She knew that coping with her grief and holiday anxiety would make her a better mother, bringing less stress and even some hope and joy to her family.

Taking time for yourself to accept and understand your grief — and give yourself permission to grieve and permission to heal — is not a selfish move. You cannot help others if you are unconscious. Put on your oxygen mask, so you can help others. I am convinced there is someone out there who needs you and wants you to be whole. Do not cheat yourself. Take care of yourself. Giving yourself permission to heal is a form of self-care.

CHAPTER 9

PHASE II: OVERCOME YOUR FEAR

Congratulations! You have learned about Phase I — Acceptance along with insights and specific tools to understand your grief, give yourself permission to grieve, and give yourself permission to heal. Now you are ready to learn about how fear becomes intertwined in grief and why it's important to understand your fear, identify your fear, and face your fear in order to overcome your fear and continue moving forward on your healing journey.

THREE PHASES TO MOVE THROUGH GRIEF TO HEALING

Phase I — Acceptance

Part 1: Understand Your Grief

Part 2: Permission to Grieve

Part 3: Permission to Heal

Phase II — Overcome Your Fear

Part 1: Understand Your Fear

Part 2: Identify Your Fear

Part 3: Face Your Fear

Phase III — Recovery

Part 1: Physical Health

Part 2: Mental Health

Part 3: Emotional Health

Part 4: Spiritual Health

For many people, fear is a significant part of the grief experience. In *A Grief Observed*, C. S. Lewis noted that grief felt very much like fear, with a sense of restlessness and similar physical sensations. I also appreciate his description that it felt as if there was an invisible blanket between him and the world.

To live in fear is an uncomfortable and debilitating way to live. Dealing with it can be absolutely exhausting and draining, especially while grieving. It can rob you of joy, peace, enthusiasm, and energy. For this reason, it is critical to overcome your fear. Ridding yourself of fear can help you learn to live fully following your loss. Regain the *you* that you lost.

What Is Fear?

Fear is the psychological reaction to danger. Fear can take root in places you never dreamed about. Fear can completely paralyze you. Fear is a natural, powerful, and primitive part of being human. There are two major responses in fear: biochemical and emotional. Fear alerts us to the presence of danger or the threat of harm, whether that danger is physical or psychological. Sometimes fear stems from real threats, but it can also originate from imagined dangers.

Ah, but fear in grief is different. Fear in grief is sinister. Fear can attack anywhere, anytime. It can grip your mind and tell you lies, causing doubt in what you feel and believe. Fear is very real in grief.

What about grief stirs your fears? You can fear your own grief, how you will handle your grief, and what you will discover about yourself and your ability to navigate your loss. It is possible grief is a new experience. It is uncharted territory.

Fear feeds on your disbelief and shock. Your ability to make sound decisions is impacted by fear. Fear can slip in and cause you to question every move, every decision, and every thought. You may feel inadequate and incompetent, having to rely on others to make even the simplest of decisions. How do you go from being fully functioning to filled with fear? After the initial shock of learning of a loved one's passing, you can experience emotional and physical fatigue, which opens the doors to foggy, unclear thinking.

Fear can be a significant part of the experience of grief. Gratefully, you are equipped with the spiritual resources to disable your fear — hope and trust. Acknowledge that fear may be inhibiting your grief recovery. Decide not to let it keep you from healing.

Signs and Symptoms of Fear

Fear often involves both physical and emotional symptoms. Each person may experience fear differently. The potential long-term consequences of fear can impact overall physical, mental, emotional, and spiritual health. The following lists present some of the most common signs and symptoms of fear.

The potential effects of fear on physical health can include:

- Headaches, migraines
- Muscle aches, body aches, chronic pain
- Difficulty breathing, asthma
- Immune system dysfunction

The potential consequences of fear on mental health can include:

- Difficulty regulating emotions
- More than usual negative thinking
- Impulsive responses
- Difficulty reading nonverbal cues
- Irrational thinking

The potential effects of fear on emotional health can include:
- Dissociation from self
- Unable to have loving feelings
- Learned helplessness
- Phobic anxiety
- Mood swings
- Obsessive-compulsive thoughts

The potential consequences of fear on spiritual health can include:

- Bitterness/fear toward God (higher power) or others
- Confusion/disgust with God (higher power) or religion
- Loss of trust in God (higher power) and/or clergy
- Waiting for God (higher power) to fix it
- Despair related to the perceived loss of spirituality

These lists are not all encompassing. It is likely that you may experience more than one of these signs and symptoms of fear as it relates to your grief.

As I noted earlier in this chapter, to live in fear is uncomfortable and debilitating. Dealing with fear can be exhausting and can rob you of enthusiasm and energy. It is critical to overcome your fear to regain hope, peace, and joy. Please keep reading. The next three chapters offer insights and specific tools to overcome your fear by:

- Understanding your fear
- Identifying your fear
- Facing your fear

CHAPTER 10

PART 1: UNDERSTAND YOUR FEAR

This chapter guides you to understand your fear. It is helpful to know that there are many types of fear including fear of letting go, fear of healing, fear of the unknown, fear of judgment, and fear of losing another loved one. As you read this chapter, think about the types of fear you may be feeling to gain a deeper understanding of your fear. This can help you to overcome your fear, so you can move through your grief to healing.

Fear of Letting Go

One of the first fears of healing through grief is letting go. It does not mean you are forgetting your love or memories of your child who has passed. To the contrary, letting go is not about your loved one, it is about you. You allow yourself to let go of your pain and suffering, which is keeping you in a deep, dark place.

You might be afraid to try something new without your loved one. You might be afraid of this change in your life, and you might feel as though you have already experienced enough change. You might be fearful of not thinking about your loved one 24/7. You might think that feeling better will dishonor them. In fact, letting go and healing is a wonderful way to show your love and respect.

I remember when I started to focus on my own journey, I sometimes felt guilty for doing so. I felt like my son would want me to think of him all the time. I felt like I would lose the memories by moving forward. As I thought about it, I realized I was creating my own fears. I discovered that creating memories was part of the healing process. It was then that I realized I would not forget Connor.

I decided to let go of my pain and suffering, instead allowing myself to think positive, good thoughts.

To put it differently, if you are binging on processed foods in your grief, you are comforted and feel good for a short period of time. To choose to not eat processed foods is to let go of the short-term effect while looking forward to feeling better in the long run by eating healthy foods.

The same with your grief. Let go of the pain and suffering, and you will experience a fulfilling life. It is about reorientating your thoughts. Once you understand that fear of letting go is something you need to face, you can start focusing more on the things you will gain instead of losing.

Do not Make them a Saint

The emotional pain I experienced after Connor died by suicide was excruciating. Initially the pain was so severe I felt like I was in a haze, in a fog that had no chance of lifting. I was in a place I did not want to be. It was challenging to perform basic functions. During the first hours, days, and weeks that followed I was in shock. As time went on the shock lifted, and I was forced to face the reality that my son was gone.

I had to come to terms with the changes in my life, almost every aspect of my daily routine. I was sometimes confused and not sure what to do next. I did know that I wanted to remember my son. Nothing was going to get in the way of that!

I started thinking about the different ways I could remember Connor. I declared to the world that I was going to start some sort of foundation in his name. It was going to be called the Tie-Dye Foundation in honor of Connor Bray Green. I had plans to have a sign made that said, "I love you to the stars and back." It was something Connor always told me when I was putting him to bed when he was little.

I spoke about him as if he were a saint, as if he never did anything wrong. Everything was about Connor. I discovered, though, that I was going too far in talking about him in such an elevated, positive manner. I turned him into a perfect person. He was not perfect. He was human and made mistakes.

I was putting Connor on a pedestal and totally forgetting about those left living in the wake of his death, especially his two sisters. I know I made them feel less valued and less loved than their brother. I can imagine their frustration in their new supporting role for their brother, the saint.

Reflecting on what was happening, I realized I was focused on the land of the dead and had moved away from the land of the living, which included my daughters, friends, and family. They were all available to support me, but Connor's "sainthood," aka his larger-than-life memory, was stopping me from staying present for those who remained.

I decided it was important to revoke his sainthood and remember the negative things as well, without being demeaning.

The trick to this was to recall his flaws and quirks with humor. We had always laughed about his tardiness and how we had to tell him dinner was an hour earlier just so he would be on time. We had laughed about him lifting his leg like a dog when he passed gas. We shared stories about how many times he had borrowed money from each of us and never paid it back. He was not perfect, yet we loved him with all his imperfections.

It is great to remember their positive qualities. It is even better to remember your loved one, quirks and all. Your child wants to be remembered as they were and not as the perfect person it is so easy to turn them into. You can hold on to their memory and honor them without sainthood.

Fear of Healing

Changing anything is difficult. The process of change itself is hard. Healing in grief is new.

In grief, you might be thinking about the time and effort it takes to heal. You could be questioning if you put in the work whether it will do you any good. Will it pay off? You could be questioning the work of journaling, meditation, exercise, or good nutrition.

In order to process your fears, you must think in advance, about how you are going to respond to them. You might be considering staying the same or doing nothing. However, staying the same serves no purpose. Be open to facing the pain, so you can heal. Going through the process of healing will help you learn to live your life without your loved one. There is hope. You can experience joy, laughter, and love while simultaneously honoring and remembering your loved one.

Remember the example of the person with the unhealthy eating habits? Instead of thinking about what they are giving up (the processed food), they can consider how they will feel by eating better. Perhaps they can cook and enjoy more at-home meals, eat more juicy and colorful fruit, and add more vegetables to their diet. Their fatigue can diminish, their focus can improve, and the quality of their sleep can skyrocket. They can overcome this particular fear of change, just as you can overcome the fear of change in your grieving process, so you can move forward, toward healing.

Fear of the Unknown

Before you start healing, you might question if you will ever experience peace, joy, and happiness again. A piece of you was lost with your loved one — will you be able to fill the void?

Rather than focusing on the negative outcomes, which by the way are a form of worry, focus on the positive. It has been proven that only a small amount of what we worry about actually happens. Do not fear the unknown. Put your energy and focus on the positive outcome you desire.

Continuing with the nutrition example, you may be that person who never tried consistently eating healthily. You may have always felt sluggish and out of shape. Changing your eating habits is something you have been told to do — but you never followed through with the advice — because feeling better is something you have not experienced. You could ask yourself, "What will the next level feel like?" Until you have experienced it, you do not know what you have been missing. Yet you can imagine feeling more energetic, alert, and healthy.

Similarly, you can ask yourself, "What will the next level feel like while on my grief journey?" Take a moment to envision a life of peace, joy, and happiness. It is within your grasp, but you cannot be afraid of the unknown. You could possibly be afraid of feeling a tidal wave of emotions and what this will do to you. You do not know what to expect. That is okay. Take the leap of faith.

Fear of Judgment

Fear of judgment, also known as social anxiety, has to do with the fear of acting in such a way in a social situation that others will judge you or develop a negative impression of you. It is an intense, persistent fear of being watched and judged by others. This fear can affect work, school, and your other day-to-day activities, especially in the face of grief.

Do you attend social gatherings and feel like you cannot mention your loved one? Possibly you have been told to "get over it" and get back to the real world.

When people are judgmental, they are often masking a lot of their own insecurities, so take a moment to think about what is going on within them. Why do they feel the need to judge you? In the case of grief, others do not know how to respond to your feelings, therefore, they project how they think you should be grieving. While this is common, it is disheartening that others do not understand what you are experiencing and cannot or do not know how to focus on being kind, patient, and supportive of you.

Fear of Losing Another Loved One (Death Anxiety)

Experiencing the loss of a loved one can increase the fear of losing someone else. Yes, it is normal to not want the people you love to die. You enjoy their company and know life would be vastly different without them.

Fear of others' death can morph into an unhealthy fear, an increase in anxiety, and extreme thinking. You spend an unhealthy amount of time thinking about how to protect your other children. Even worse, you question how you will ever live without them — although they are still living. This can bring dread and overwhelm caused by irrational thoughts and behaviors.

The reality is that loss is inevitable.

Also, we do not talk enough about death in our modern culture. So there can be a certain amount of fear simply because you do not fully know what you would be dealing with if another loved one died.

Sigmund Freud coined fear of death and dying as *thanatophobia* and believed that everyone suffers from it, because we refuse to accept our mortality. Modern psychologists call this common fear *death anxiety*.

The more time you spend dwelling on losing another loved one, the worse you can feel. Anxiety, illogical thinking, rapid breathing, disrupted sleep and eating patterns, and panic attacks are possible symptoms of focusing on a future loss. You might even dwell on your own mortality.

It is important to remember that death is inevitable, and no matter how hard you try, you cannot change that it will happen to everyone including you, sometime, somewhere, and somehow.

Review the five types of fear presented in this chapter and take a moment now to make a list of the fear you may be facing. You may experience one or more of these fears. You will use this list in the following chapters where we discuss identifying your fear and facing your fear.

How you choose to see things dictates how you experience them. Would you rather see everything as precious or pointless? Stop dwelling on the inevitable and enjoy the time you have with your loved ones. Go out and create memories. Today.

CHAPTER 11

PART 2: IDENTIFY YOUR FEAR

Fear is a common experience among those who are grieving. No matter how strong you think you are, fear can creep in. The reality is that you can overcome most fear, once you contemplate it and understand what it actually is.

Fear can compound with one event on top of another. Be mindful when fear surfaces. Stop, pause, and ask yourself, "When was the first time I remember feeling this emotion? What was happening in my life?" A memory may surface, and you can look at this objectively and ask yourself, "What did I learn from this memory that will allow me to let go of the emotions associated with it?"

By allowing these uncomfortable feelings to play out and understand where they originate, they will start to dissipate much more quickly than if you were to avoid them.

In the following pages, you will ask yourself some deep and possibly uncomfortable questions will that help to identify your fear even further. Use these questions to start peeling away the layers of the onion to further identify your fear (or fears) that you listed in the previous chapter.

Sometimes you might encounter upsetting situations. Knowing the truth can help to alleviate your fear. For example, if you hate hearing loud music and it makes you fearful, anxious, and even angry, you might think you are upset at the loudness. But if you dig deeper, you may discover that your fear and other strong feelings come from the trigger that your loved one played their music loud, causing you to miss them and suddenly feel overwhelmed with deep sadness.

Below are a few questions you can use to identify when and where your fear raises its ugly head. Be sure to write down your responses — this insight will be useful as you read the rest of this chapter and the next chapter. While answering these questions, keep in mind the five types of fear we discussed in the previous chapter: fear of letting go, fear of healing, fear of the unknown, fear of judgment, and fear of losing another loved one. Take time to carefully think about each question and your answer. This will help you gain a deeper understanding of your fear (or fears), further identify which fear you are experiencing, learn what triggers your fear, and clarify your emotional responses when you experience fear. These insights will empower you to overcome your fear.

Questions to Further Identify Your Fear

1. **What, in that moment, triggered your fear?** What made you fearful? Was it a memory, event, or something that was said?

2. **What is a fear that you had prior to your loss?** Perhaps it is setting the stage for how you respond to your fear now.

3. **Have you avoided certain jobs, people, places, situations, conversations, or experiences out of a fear of something?** What was the fear? Is this avoidance based in a deeper fear?

4. **Does it make you uncomfortable to talk about your loved one?** Why? Which fear is stopping you?

5. **Do you fear taking a step forward?** What is stopping you?

6. **Do you fear the truth?** Are you afraid of hearing the truth? Why?

7. **Are you comfortable with being vulnerable?** If no, why not? Can you pinpoint a deeper fear?

8. **Are you afraid of what other people think of you?** What about this scares you most?

9. **Does uncertainty and "not knowing" scare you or make you feel uncomfortable?** What about it scares you?

10. **How do you feel about change?** Does it scare you? What about it scares you?

11. **Are you choosing to be alone in order to hide from others?** If so, what deeper fear is it based in?

12. **Are you choosing to spend most of your time keeping busy so that you avoid facing your grief?** If so, what deeper fear is it based in?

You will more than likely feel extremely uncomfortable and procrastinate in identifying your fear (or fears). It is important to do this — let your uncomfortable thoughts surface. The more you know about your fears, the less scary they are. With this information in hand, look back at your written answers to the above questions. You have now identified your deepest fears and have gained more insights about them. This takes one aspect of fear out of play: fear of the unknown.

Signs that Fear Is Running How You Grieve

- *You say yes when you mean no* — When you are afraid to disappoint people or get rejected if you do not say yes, you will fall into fear-based, people-pleasing, self-sacrificing behaviors that can lead to resentment. You can fully be hiding your emotions and leading on to others that you are okay. But when fear is no longer running the show, you can say no when it feels self-loving. "No" is a complete sentence. This does not mean you will not devote yourself to generosity and service. You can be discerning about what you say yes to.

- *You say no when you mean yes* — When you are afraid, you are unlikely to take risks or even take small, healthy steps forward. You will feel the yearning to move forward in your grief. Deep-down inside you want to join friends for dinner or take that weekend getaway trip, but you will say no, because you are afraid to be judged, have fun, and get out of your comfort zone.

- **_You numb with food, alcohol, technology, or busyness_** — Fear and grief cause inner pain, which is easy to numb with substances and behaviors. But these are only a temporary Band-Aid on the pain and ultimately decrease your self-esteem and ability to move through your grief in the long run. When you are not afraid to be quiet with yourself, face your inner feelings, and heal from the core, you will no longer need the distractions. You will have the courage to do the transformative work that leads you to freedom on the other side of your journey.

- **_You procrastinate_** — When you are afraid to walk the path to healing, you tend to watch life pass by where you feel safe. When you face fear head-on and are open to experiencing peace, joy, and happiness, this renewed energy will replace the desire to put things off.

- **_You find it difficult to make a decision_** — When fear is running your life, you avoid making decisions, some of them basic life decisions. You know from your inner core that you have the experience and knowledge to decide what is next but find that you have self-doubt in the simplest decisions.

- **_You are sick_** — Fear is not just the emotional and mental response. It can trigger physical responses, lower your immunity, and put you at an increased risk of disease. As you will learn later in this book, your physical health is just as important in healing your grief as mental, emotional, and spiritual health.

Signs That Fear Is Holding You Back

- *You only see the downside* — Fear lets you see only the negative, and that will not get you far. You tend to identify only the worst thing that can happen. You turn down opportunities to experience new things to move forward in your grief.

- *You have a fight or flight response* — Fear does not let you stop to think. It initiates a fight or flight response that forces you to react quickly. However, you have the option to analyze your choices. Unless the circumstances are life threatening, you can stop and think about your situation (and your reaction to it), even if just for a few moments.

- *Your world gets smaller* — Fear makes your world smaller. In grief, instead of reaching out for help or tapping into your tribe, you choose to withdraw. You have a limited number of people you can turn to. Your social interactions may diminish. As a result of your smaller world, you feel lost and alone in your grief.

- *Your intuition is stunted* — Fear alters what Mother Nature has given you: intuition. There is no room for that small, still voice when fear is present. All you can hear are the spiraling thoughts coursing through your mind. When you are consumed with fear, your gut instincts are hard, if not impossible, to recognize.

- *You are paralyzed and cannot make decisions* — Fear can also paralyze you and keep you from making any decision. A wise person once said, "Choose a path, or a path will be chosen for you." Fear keeps you second-guessing yourself and, thus, you avoid making decisions.

Why Is It Important To Identify Your Fear?

At the most basic level, you cannot overcome a fear if you do not increase your awareness of it by identifying it. Fear, in general, takes place through the mechanism of unconscious thought. Therefore, the solution is to bring conscious awareness into the equation.

Take a few minutes to review your answers to the questions in this chapter. Also, did you make a list of your fears in Chapter 10? If not, please do so now. Keep this information handy since we will build on these insights in the following chapter. As a reminder, the five types of fear are:

- Fear of letting go
- Fear of healing
- Fear of the unknown
- Fear of judgment
- Fear of losing another loved one

Remember, if you do not identify your fear, it controls you. Do you want to be in control of your fear, or do you want your fear to control you? Ask yourself, "Why am I letting it rule me? How much does it rule me?" This is a choice you must make.

CHAPTER 12

PART 3: FACE YOUR FEAR

Nothing good comes out of allowing your fear to rule your thoughts, actions, and behaviors. Instead, you must learn how to become skillful at the art of exposing your deepest fear, facing your fear, and being able to take the next step to overcome it. As a reminder, there are three steps in Phase II — Overcome Your Fear: understanding your fear, identifying your fear, and facing your fear. Each is a vital step on your path to heal.

How can you face your fear? Why is it important to do so? Let's start with a real-life story to illustrate how this step can help you to move forward on your healing journey.

Kathi's Story

Kathi was late joining her Zoom coaching session. This was out of the ordinary for her. Normally she was early to her coaching call and ready to dive into her homework. But this past week's homework was about identifying her fear. Remember, fear can be a significant part of your grief experience. It can hold you back from stepping into your new norm and purpose. It is not an easy concept to grasp.

Kathi finally popped into our session. She apologized for being late and admitted this week's topic of fear made her unusually uncomfortable. She was confused and really did not know what to think. I told her it was okay and to give herself grace about not knowing how to handle this week's subject. She would be learning some tools that would help her.

As our session progressed, Kathi admitted that she was finding it extremely difficult to make the smallest decisions. When the family was choosing where to go to dinner, she was unable to voice an opinion or offer any input. She expressed frustration over making a simple choice.

She realized that fear was getting in her way. She was frozen, and she feared that any decision would be the wrong one and everything would turn out poorly. Prior to her daughter's death, Kathi was decisive, confident, and determined. She did not like living fearfully.

To help identify her deepest fear, I asked her, "What is causing you to feel this way?" She answered my simple question by saying she did not like what others thought of her. I followed with, "Do you fear that others are judging you?" Immediately she shouted, "Yes! That was it!" She feared others would judge her for being in public and not being at home mourning, especially if she was laughing and enjoying herself.

Kathi also thought others even blamed her for her daughter's death. Because of the fear of judgment, she did not want to face anyone, not even strangers. This fear of judgment was making it difficult for Kathi to make other decisions. It was a dark cloud that followed her everywhere.

I asked Kathi if she was assuming that these other people were judging her. Another yes response. She interpreted their smile as a sneer, their look as condescending, and their tone of voice as platitude. As we dug deeper, she discovered these were stories she was making up without any facts to substantiate them.

One tool to overcome fear and doubt is by making small decisions and sticking to them. Kathi said she found it difficult to choose an outfit for work, wondering who would judge her at the office. Together, we decided she would choose an outfit the night before, and the next morning she would get up, knowing what she would be wearing. She would not have to think about it. It was simple. If any doubt did creep in, she would say this affirmation: "I am confident of my decision. I made a good choice." She also would repeat, "I do not let fear run my life."

As we wrapped up our time together, Kathi felt better. She identified her fear of judgment and was able to put strategies in place to overcome it.

Name Your Deepest Fear

With the list of fears you identified in the previous chapters, it is now time to give life to each fear by giving it a name. For example, you may have decided that you fear losing another loved one. Personify it by naming it. Any name will do. You may choose something such as Debbie Downer, Angry Adam, or Sad Susie. Do this with each fear identified on your list.

If you recall, Kathi identified one of her deepest fears as the fear of being judged. She then named it Judgmental Judy. Every time Judgmental Judy came around, Kathi was able to tell her "No thank you" and use her affirmations to subdue this fear. The fear of being judged gradually lost its grip on her.

By giving fear a name, it increases your awareness. You cannot overcome a fear that you are not aware of and controls you. Instead, you can learn how to become skillful in exposing your fear and using the following coping mechanisms to overcome it.

The best way to get rid of your fear is to find techniques that will help you identify the true source of your fear and manage your response. If you can do this, then you should be able to overcome any fears and anxieties. The following pages present several tools and techniques to help you face your fear. I encourage you to try them all and, of course, take what you like and leave the rest.

Learn from Your Own Past and Present Experience

Take note when fear surfaces and then also notice what you did to get through it. In your journal write down what worked for you and what did not. For example, when the fear of being judged surfaces, you can utilize the box breathing technique you will learn later in this chapter. Keep track of the positive experience by writing it down. Do this so the next time you experience this fear, or any fear, you can remind yourself to use the same tool.

List What You Have Already Lost

The purpose of this step is not to drudge up old pain but to help you recognize that you are probably more resilient than you realize.

Write out things that you valued and lost, whether a friend moved away, a relationship ended, or the loss of a parent or sibling occurred. Draw upon your memory to remember what you did to navigate through that loss and how you bounced back, healed, or recovered. Be sure to write this down in your journal.

Breathe through Your Fear

One symptom of facing fear is an increased heart rate. If you experience this stay calm and understand it will pass. If symptoms persist, seek medical care. One tool to use when fear raises its ugly head is to use your breathing to minimize the impact fear has on you.

You can practice deep breathing to slow your heart rate. The goal is to learn and apply coping skills when fear arises. With coping techniques in hand, fear loses its power over you.

Try the box breathing technique: Think of your breathing pattern as a box. In the upper-left corner of your imaginary box draw a horizontal line to the right; this line represents your inhalation. Now draw a vertical line straight down; this represents your exhalation. The third line goes horizontally to the left, representing your second inhalation. The next line is vertical (straight up), representing your second exhalation and connecting to the original starting point. You have now created a box pattern to complete your breathwork. Each side of your breathing box — inhalation and exhalation — is done to a count of four.

Follow these four simple steps to complete one round of box breathing:

1. Take a deep long breath in, count to four slowly while pushing the fresh air deep down into your lungs so that your belly expands. (First horizontal line.)
2. As you exhale, empty your lungs and belly while counting to four. (First vertical line.)
3. Take a deep, long breath in, count to four slowly while pushing the fresh air deep down into your lungs so that your belly expands. (Second horizontal line.)
4. As you exhale, empty your lungs and belly while counting to four. (Second vertical line.)

Complete five to ten rounds of box breathing to reduce your fear and anxiety. Breathing like this can slow down your heart rate, clear your thoughts, and take away your fear.

Use this box breathing technique when you are feeling fearful, have anxiety, run into a stressful situation, or feel that life has gotten too heavy. You can also use it as prevention. For example, if you are struggling with going to the grocery store, use this technique before leaving the house. You may want to repeat it in your car before going into the store, and you can even do it while in the store. Do this box breathing technique often and wherever you need it.

Box Breathing Technique

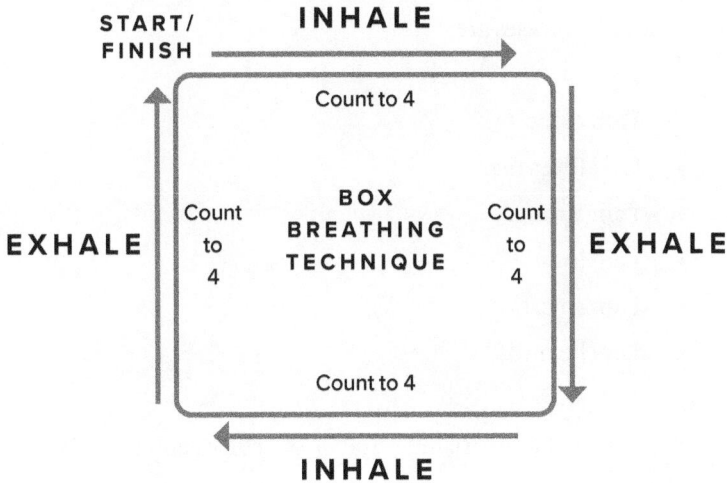

Visualize a Happy Place

Take a moment and close your eyes. In your mind, take yourself to a place where you feel safe and calm. You could be walking on a beach, sitting in a chair watching the sunset, or snuggling with your happy kitty. Let that feeling wash over you until your fear has subsided. The more you do this, the less frequently your fear will appear.

Meditate

Meditation is a well-studied and proven way to reduce fear, helping to take away the signs and symptoms of fear as well. You can start with just a few minutes a day and work your way up to as long of an experience as you want.

You may even have heard that you need to be a monk, not speak to anyone, and isolate yourself deep in a forest. While that is an option to meditate, it is certainly not required! Meditation can be as simple as repeating a phrase or humming a tune over and over. Some sample phrases are:

- I am okay.
- God loves me.
- I am strong.
- I am loved.
- I am smart.
- I am beautiful.

You can find a surprising number of articles about meditation and guidance to meditate in the manner that suits you best on the Internet. Plus, you can explore the wide variety of easy-to-use, downloadable apps that can help you meditate.

Question What and How You Think

Each time a fear-based thought enters your head, you have a choice. You can accept it as the story you believe, or you can question it and think about it differently.

Ask yourself, "Is this really true?" If not, then ask yourself, "How can I think about this thought differently?" Consider that it does not serve you, and you will not allow it to seep into your consciousness. Replace it with another thought that serves you in the moment.

For example, when Debbie Downer or Angry Adam come to visit, you have a choice regarding how you think about them. You have the power to tell them to go away, and you have the power to replace those fear-based thoughts with positive thoughts.

Trust in Your Higher Power

When you believe it is a hostile universe, life is scary. But when you trust that you are held, loved, safe, nurtured, and protected, you can relax. Whether you subscribe to a specific religion or just consider yourself to be spiritual but not religious, anything that facilitates your trust in a friendly universe can help you to move beyond fear.

Use the techniques mentioned earlier in the chapter as your fear arises. Use them separately or in conjunction with each other. Find what works for you, so you can move forward on your journey and banish your fear.

Give Yourself Grace

Finally, if you have a day when fear takes you down and out of commission, give yourself grace and remind yourself that this a journey. There will be good days, bad days, and setbacks. However, for the most part, you are moving forward in your journey toward hope and healing — and focusing on the light of laughter, joy, and enjoyment.

CHAPTER 13

PHASE III: RECOVERY

I n grief, it is all too easy to turn to unhealthy behaviors such as alcohol, drugs, overeating, and binge-watching TV, but these behaviors do not serve you. Now is the time to focus on the healthy choices you can make in self-care including getting restorative sleep, drinking plenty of water, getting outdoors, and spending time with friends and family.

Here, in Phase III — Recovery, we focus on the importance of healing your health in grief. The following chapters address the four parts of recovery: healing your physical, mental, emotional, and spiritual health.

THREE PHASES TO MOVE
THROUGH GRIEF TO HEALING

Phase I — Acceptance

Part 1: Understand Your Grief

Part 2: Permission to Grieve

Part 3: Permission to Heal

Phase II — Overcome Your Fear

Part 1: Understand Your Fear

Part 2: Identify Your Fear

Part 3: Face Your Fear

Phase III — Recovery

Part 1: Physical Health

Part 2: Mental Health

Part 3: Emotional Health

Part 4: Spiritual Health

As you learn about the four areas of health — physical, mental, emotional, and spiritual — you will find there are multiple modalities for each health component. I recommend experiencing many of them at least once. You may find that a particular combination of modalities helps you the most. I have personally experienced these tools and recommendations, and I know they work.

You will notice an obvious absence of traditional Western medicine. There are plenty of resources available on the Internet and via traditional sources such as your physician or counselors, psychiatrists, and psychologists who focus on talk therapy and other Western modalities. However, I have found that practical, proven information encompassing "wholistic" grief healing is much more limited, and that is why I focus on bringing you these options. The following four chapters focus on recovery by healing your physical health, mental health, emotional health, and spiritual health.

CHAPTER 14

PART 1: PHYSICAL HEALTH

P hysical health is often overlooked in the grief healing process. Due to the traumatic nature of a child's death by suicide, it is even more important to address physical health. It is a barometer that indicates how things are going in all areas of your health.

Poor physical health symptoms caused by grief may include fatigue, restlessness, migraines, insomnia, extreme weight gain or weight loss, chronic pain and inflammation, diabetes, heart attack, stroke, high blood pressure, and broken heart syndrome. Grief can also weaken your immune system, making you prone to colds, flu, and an increased risk of autoimmune diseases. You may be experiencing one or many of these symptoms right now.

What does good physical health look like? Your physical body is the reflection and total sum of all aspects of who you are. Without

SURVIVE YOUR CHILD'S SUICIDE

it, you will fail to thrive. Physical health is foundational in easing complications of grief and promoting healing. There are a variety of things you can do for your physical health such as sleep, meditation, hydration, nutrition, and exercise.

In this chapter, you will learn how to identify poor physical health and improve it to help you move through your grief to healing.

Importance of Physical Health

I combined my personal training, nutrition consulting, and wellness coaching experience to bring this chapter to you. This is my favorite topic!

Stress caused by grief and suffering will wreak havoc on your body if you do not do something to prevent it. In your grief, it is easy to stop taking care of yourself. When you no longer give your body the care it needs, it will shut down. Grief is physical.

In Chinese medicine, grief is associated with the lungs. The lungs are responsible for breathing, which can break down in stressful times. It is not a coincidence that after a difficult period, people catch colds or get bronchitis or pneumonia. Your immune system is compromised, leaving you susceptible to illness, colds, cases of flu, and even cancer.

I have seen the impact of emotional stress and grief on my father and sister. As I mentioned, they both passed away from cancer. I cannot help but see the correlation between their stress-filled lives, their diagnosis and ultimate passing from cancer.

While I cannot scientifically prove that stress caused their cancer, I can scientifically prove that free radicals are caused by stress. Free radicals are unstable atoms that float around in your body, looking for a home. When they cannot find a home, they damage the cells around them. Damaged cells can no longer fight off diseases such as cold, flu, and short-term fatigue. Longer-term impacts can include diabetes, heart attack, stroke, cancer, autoimmune diseases, arthritis, poor memory, wrinkles, and in extreme cases death. These mutated cells replicate time and time again, making it harder and harder to bring your body back to homeostasis or equilibrium.

As a mother who has lost two children, I decided I did not want to put my remaining children through the horrifying experience of watching me suffer through cancer or other illnesses. When my son passed away, I knew I was in for a long ride of stress — stress that, if I did not handle it properly, could have taken over my life, possibly killing me.

I am fortunate that my education and practical experience came in handy in this stress-filled time. I was able to go on autopilot regarding my physical health. I knew what to do from my many years of practicing personal training and focusing on health and wellness. If I was going to survive this season, I had to take care of myself.

What Is Self-Care?

What does self-care look like? Self-care is what you do deliberately for physical, mental, emotional, and spiritual wellbeing. In this chapter, I focus on physical health, which is often the most ignored, denied, and disregarded. However, it is an important piece in your recovery and should not be overlooked. Self-care is part of that package of total wellbeing and moving through grief to healing, so you can live a fulfilling life brimming with peace, joy, and happiness.

As a mother, you are a caregiver. It is natural to want to take care of others. I believe the desire to nurture is inborn and makes it who you are. That nurturing instinct is also what makes your grief so deep and wide. Once a child is placed in your hands, they have your heart forever. You have a child to love and take care of. They are small, fragile, and incapable of self-care. You take on that responsibility with joy and gladness, teaching them how to take care of their needs.

The first time your child picks up a small piece of food and puts it in their mouth you rejoice. You teach them how to eat. You teach them how to use the potty, wear a coat, and soothe themselves when hurt. Self-care is something they learn from you, and you encourage them to continue to learn this throughout their life.

Often, you focus so much on nurturing others that your own health takes a backseat. It is easy to get wrapped up in the wellbeing of your children. When they are taken from you there is a big, gaping hole in your heart. You do not know what to do or how to take care of yourself or even why it should be done.

Taking care of your needs is not a guilty pleasure. The mixed messages you get as a mother come from within and from others. I have seen women be judged, because they take time to exercise, play a favorite sport, meditate, or simply take time for themselves. They are told they should be at home with their children. Guilt and shame are placed on their shoulders. They fall into the trap of pleasing others and doing what others think they should be doing.

If you are a mom who tells yourself that you do not have time to exercise, play, or meditate, it is time to focus on you. It is okay to take care of yourself. It is time to do what you need to do for you.

Exercise

Regular, whole-body exercise can have a profoundly positive impact on depression, anxiety, and grief. It also relieves stress, improves memory, helps you sleep better, and boosts your overall mood. It can help with weight management, improve your ability to focus, and offer a sense of control. And you do not have to be a fitness fanatic to reap the benefits!

As a personal trainer for twelve years, I have helped hundreds of clients reach strength and weight-loss goals. I have also seen the impact exercise had on several mothers who lost a child. It is not a coincidence that I helped these mothers through their loss.

Ignoring your physical health will not make it go away and definitely will not make it better. As a matter of fact, the longer you deny your health the higher the risk of more extensive physical challenges. Unresolved grief can manifest into complicated health challenges and mental illness.

There are three basic types of exercise: aerobic, strength training, and stretching. They are all important components of your health. If you are new to exercise, please remember to consult with your physician before beginning any exercise routine.

Aerobic Exercise

Also known as cardiovascular exercise, aerobic exercise can help reduce the risk of cardiovascular disease and heal cardiovascular damage, some of which may be associated with broken heart syndrome. Aerobic exercise can also lower blood pressure and raise your good cholesterol levels while lowering the bad levels. Cardio can also reduce chronic pain, help with sleep, and improve focus.

All of these are great benefits of getting your heart pumping. One I have not mentioned, though, is boosting your mood with the feel-good endorphins. They help to reduce your stress and elevate your heart rate, which can help release anger and guilt.

The U.S. Centers for Disease Control and Prevention (CDC) recommends that American adults get at least 150 minutes of moderate-to-intensive aerobic activity every week. Moderate-to-intensive activity will raise your heart rate and make you breathe faster and feel warmer. If you can easily have a conversation but cannot sing a song, then you are working out at a moderate level.

Some examples of moderate-to-intensive aerobic activities include:

- Brisk walking
- Jogging or running
- Playing tennis
- Water aerobics
- Swimming
- Riding a bike
- Dancing
- Pushing a lawn mower
- Hiking
- Roller blading

Another option is to get seventy-five minutes of vigorous intensity activity each week. Vigorous intensity activity makes you breathe hard and fast. If you are working at this level, you may not be able to say more than a few words without pausing to breathe.

Vigorous intensity activities include:

- Running or skipping
- Swimming
- Riding a bike fast or up hills
- Sports: basketball, rugby, lacrosse
- Aerobics class
- Martial arts

If you exercised prior to experiencing a loved one's death, you may feel good about returning to the same intensity level. You may already be familiar with having endorphins pumped into your body, giving you more energy, greater clarity, and a stronger immune system. You understand the increased levels of serotonin that help you to sleep and the reduced cortisol that decreases stress. If this describes your exercise routine, I recommend you keep doing it.

However, if you are not acquainted with the benefits of exercise, I want to encourage you to start. Please remember to consult your physician before starting any exercise routine.

I find that many people who have never exercised before begin with walking. The recommendation is to reach 10,000 steps a day. You can download an app on your phone or buy a fitness tracker. If you do not know how many steps you generally get every day, keep track for three days: two weekdays and one weekend day. Take an average and then add 10 percent as a starting daily goal. Each week add 5 to 10 percent in steps to keep increasing your goal until you reach about 10,000 steps a day. Doing this can help to increase energy, improve your mood, and reduce inflammation.

Brenda's Experience with Exercise

Brenda started working with me after her twenty-nine-year-old son took his life. She could not believe I recommended that she get off the couch and out of the house. She felt like I was trying to force her into something she did not want to do. She was struggling with even the thought of walking out the door.

I suggested she start by setting a goal of walking around the block as part of her daily morning routine. She committed to doing her best for one week. She logged her activity every day and noted how she felt after she walked. When we met the following week, Brenda felt lighter. She admitted walking had improved her mood, and she had more energy.

Exercise is also a good way to connect with others and avoid isolation. You may choose to exercise outdoors with others, spending time with those who support you. Being outdoors is also a place to ground yourself and connect with nature.

Aerobic exercise is an important piece to total health healing as a suicide loss survivor. You can choose one or several modes of exercise. Remember, exercise helps to increase energy, improve your mood, reduce inflammation, reduce risk of autoimmune disease, lower risk of heart attack, and improve your shattered heart.

Strength Training for Health

The second type of exercise I want to discuss is strength training. While I am unaware of specific research studies on suicide loss survivors and bone density, there is a study that correlates the death of spouse to an increased risk of hip fractures. Medicines used to treat depression such as selective serotonin reuptake inhibitors (SSRIs) are associated with a 70 percent increase in falls and fractures. Stressful life events are also associated with a loss of bone mass in the hip, falls, and fractures. My hypothesis is that suicide as a stressful life event will result in similar findings. I am not a researcher, but I do know it is worth doing strength training to reduce risk of bone density loss and fractures if you take a fall.

According to the American College of Sports Medicine, it is recommended that women complete whole-body workouts two to three times a week. Lifting free weights, using resistance machines, or doing exercises to lift your own body weight are different types of strength training.

The mental attention it takes to focus on the muscles being worked trains your mind to do something different. Strength training can be a temporary distraction to your problems and an opportunity to channel your energy for positive outcomes. Strength training also is an outlet for built-up energy. Lifting heavy things can be soothing for your soul. To ensure you are using equipment and doing the exercises properly I recommend working one-on-one with a personal trainer.

Stretching in Grief

Stretching is the third type of physical exercise and is particularly important when dealing with grief. It is common to carry tension in your neck and shoulders. You might experience jaw pain from excessive muscle tension, tooth discomfort from grinding, headaches, and overall body aches.

When Suzanne came to me, she was incredibly tense. She was unable to look over her shoulder to check traffic when driving. To see what was in her blind spot, she had to rotate her entire upper body instead of simply moving her head. She also complained that she woke up every morning with severe headaches. To get her day started, she took over-the-counter pain medication, which seemed to help less and less. She became agitated quickly and physically felt horrible.

I recommended that she visit a specialty pillow store to ensure her neck and head were receiving the correct support while she slept. She invested in a new pillow and gained a small amount of relief. That was a good starting point, but I knew we needed to do more. I suggested a simple routine of seven exercises that she could do in under three minutes. They do not require special equipment and can be done anywhere, any time, and multiple times during the day.

While these stretching exercises are short and simple, do not underestimate their power. Just after one week of practicing them, Suzanne saw a noticeable difference in her ability to rotate her head. Plus, her headaches were less severe in the morning. She stopped taking the pain medication and was not so cranky in the morning.

Here are the exercises. In this series of neck stretches, it is best to be sitting in a chair with both feet on the ground. Do each exercise for thirty seconds to ease the tension. Take each move to feeling the stretch, but do not stretch into pain. Your neck is a vulnerable area of your body, and it is easy to overdo it. Remember to stretch gently.

1. Alternate looking over each shoulder, just as if you are checking traffic while driving.
2. Look up to the ceiling and look down to the floor, tucking your chin to your chest.

3. Jut your chin forward then bring your head back to expose the jowls of your neck.

4. Roll your head in a half-circle on your chest.

5. Alternate drawing each ear up and away from your shoulder to the ceiling.

6. Keep your eyes focused forward and move your head side to side, like an Egyptian hieroglyph.

7. Open your mouth as wide as you can then bring your lips to a pucker.

In addition to these neck exercises, I recommended that Suzanne participate in yoga. There are several types of yoga, and you will find one that works for you. You can participate in classes in person at local yoga studios or gyms or online (check out the many YouTube videos).

Exercise is an important piece to total health healing as a suicide survivor. I suggest you combine a little of each one of these components: aerobic exercise, strength training, and stretching. Receive videos of free classes including low-intensity aerobic exercise, high-intensity interval training, Pilates, yoga, and meditation exercises by going to my website, www.TheGriefSpecialist.com, and clicking on the Self-Care in Grief tab.

People always ask me this question, "Peggy, what is the best exercise?" I tell them the best exercise is the one you will do and be consistent with. So just get started.

Let us now transition and discuss the role nutrition plays in physical health and your grief journey.

Nutrition and Physical Health

In times of stress, you will more than likely crave foods that are high in fat, sugar, and salt. It is extremely easy to grab cookies or chips and use unhealthy processed foods as a way to make you feel better. Yes, they make you feel better in the short term, however, in the long run they make you feel so much worse. They affect your blood sugar, your energy level, and your mental focus.

In addition, heavy amounts of cortisol, the stress hormone, are released during times of stress and contribute to weight gain. And without a doubt, processed foods can add unwanted calories. Processed foods are also attributed to weakening your immune system, opening the floodgates to simple colds, more severe heart conditions, and oxidative stress. Oxidative stress damages your cells and can contribute to autoimmune diseases and cancer.

I want to share with you what healthy eating looks like. Ultimately the goal is to follow this as closely as possible. However, give yourself some grace if you do not. Nutrition is about health and wellness as part of your grief and healing. Pay attention to your gut. Foods high in trans fats, excess calories, additives, and salt contribute to inflammation and affect your gut health. Your gut is considered to be your "second brain" and contributes to your emotional and mental wellness.

When grieving or feeling stressed, anxious, or sad focus on keeping up with a well-balanced diet. There are seven components to a well-balanced diet. You will add more real food and water. Reduce or eliminate gluten and dairy. Finally, reduce caffeine, alcohol, and sugar.

Today, I am offering you a framework for good nutritional habits and healing in grief. There is so much I would love to share with you. Let us start with the first two suggestions: what you are adding to your diet.

Eat Real Food

Times of stress and grieving cause the body to be more inflamed. It is important that during this period you do everything you can to get your inflammatory load down. That can be accomplished by eating real food. Real food does not come in boxes, cans, or microwave containers. It comes from the earth.

It is recommended to eat nine to thirteen servings of fruits and vegetables a day. Simple carbohydrates such as fruits and vegetables provide the vitamins, minerals, and antioxidants that your body needs.

Whole foods have specific health benefits associated with them:

- Dark, leafy-green vegetables such as spinach, arugula, mustard greens, Swiss chard, and kale offer nutrients that decrease inflammation, enhance immune function, provide energy, and provide necessary fiber.
- Blueberries, strawberries, raspberries, and blackberries can help with memory and provide vitamin C for anti-inflammatory properties and immune support.
- Sweet potatoes pack a punch of anti-inflammatory nutrients that optimize immune response and add another layer of protection.
- Nuts and seeds such as almonds, pecans, walnuts, sunflower seeds, and hemp seeds provide plant-based protein and healthy fats. They act as an antioxidant in your body,

protecting against cellular damage. Remember, cell damage is caused by stress, and unhealthy, damaged cells leave your body's system open for autoimmune diseases, cancer, and other chronic illnesses.

- Fruits such as apples, oranges, mangos, pineapples, peaches, and cherries are a good source of vitamin C, fiber, potassium, and folate. They are naturally sweet and can satisfy cravings.

- Foods rich in magnesium help to reduce the production of cortisol, the stress hormone that causes inflammation. You may find some of these are your favorites: avocados, bananas, broccoli, pumpkin seeds, and dark chocolate. Remember though, enjoy chocolate in moderation.

- Salmon is a wonderful source of healthy fatty acids, which promote brain, joint, eye, and heart health.

I understand eating may be difficult, let alone eating more fruits and vegetables. That is why I have been eating Juice Plus+ plant-based powder in a capsule for years. These capsules include the nutritional benefits of 30 different fruits and vegetables such as spinach, kale, broccoli, raspberries, blueberries, apple, peaches, and mango. This makes it easy for me to fill the nutritional gap. It gives me the nutrition of the vitamins, minerals, and antioxidants that I do not get when I'm not eating like I should. This has helped me to stay healthy during my stressful season, along with my other healthy lifestyle choices.

The day after Connor died, I doubled-up on my Juice Plus+. Knowing the damage stress has on the body, I wanted to be proactive and protect myself, because I did not want what happened to my dad and sister to happen to me. Both of them died of cancer shortly after extremely stressful life events. God willing, I was not going to let that happen to me. I have two daughters and grandchildren to live for. Now more than ever, they need me.

For additional information on Juice Plus+, please visit my website, www.TheGriefSpecialist.com, and click on the Self-Care in Grief tab.

Drink Water

Dehydration is a special danger for bereaved parents because the shock of their losses often leaves them stunned, powerless to focus on their needs, and without energy. They may also experience general loss of motivation, general aches and pains, or headaches.

Your body is 60 percent water, and your organs need water to function properly. Your heart and brain both are 73 percent water, your skin is 64 percent water, and your bones are 31 percent water. It is no wonder that when your body is dehydrated your thinking is clouded and you cannot focus. In grief you may even feel that your heart is literally breaking. In the grief work I have done I often hear the comment that people feel like they have aged ten years, or they often have difficulty breathing. Listen to your body. Your organs are crying out that they need attention and desperately need water. When you do not replenish what you use, your organs can shut down.

You also need water to detoxify your body and flush out the toxins that accumulate from stress, anxiety, and grief. During stress you produce extra toxins that can stay in your system. The only way to get rid of them is to drink water. And I mean water. Coffee, tea, sodas, and alcohol do not replace water.

It is recommended to drink one-half of your body weight in ounces of water. In your grief, that is the minimum to get on a daily basis.

It is easy to calculate how much water you should be drinking every day. Here is an example: If you weigh 120 pounds, divide 120 by 2, which is 60. This means your body requires 60 ounces of water, at a minimum, to stay hydrated and functioning and help with your grief.

Now is the time to focus on your health and drink more water. It is an easy place to start.

A common reaction is, "Whoa, that is a lot of water, and I will be spending my days in the restroom. I do not have time for that." You are correct; initially you will be using the restroom frequently. Think of your body as a bone-dry sponge. If you pour a lot of water on a dried-up sponge, most of the water will run right off. As you continue to add more water, the sponge will retain more and more water. You are like that! Your body will get used to having more water, and the need to use the restroom will diminish.

Now, calculate your water-drinking goal. Your body weight in pounds = ____ /2 = ____ ounces of water to drink daily. Set this amount as a goal to drink every day. Write it down here so you remember.

My water intake goal is _____ ounces every day.

Look for increased energy, better sleep, and clearer thinking as you add more water to your daily routine.

The next three recommendations address what I suggest you remove from your diet.

Reduce or Eliminate Gluten

What is gluten and why should you avoid it? Gluten is a general name for the proteins found in wheat, rye, and barley. Gluten helps foods maintain their shape, acting as a glue that holds food together. I am not sure about you, but I do not like the idea of eating glue. Gluten provides no essential nutrients. Gluten and its byproducts are commonly found in processed foods such as bread, pasta, pizza, and cereal.

Gluten is inflammatory and adds to the natural inflammatory response caused by grief.

Gluten can have serious consequences to your microbiome and for those with celiac disease. The microbiome is a collection of friendly bacteria that lives in your gut. These friendly bacteria help to regulate your immune system and control digestion. Gluten may be responsible for stomach pain, irritable bowel syndrome, and bloating.

It can also cause brain fog (also known as grief brain), increased fatigue, and higher risk of autoimmune diseases and may contribute to depression. When it all adds up, gluten does not serve you, especially in grief. It really is beneficial to your physical and mental health to remove gluten from your diet.

Reduce or Eliminate Dairy

One of the health concerns from dairy is that milk contains hormones, even organic milk. Cows produce the stress hormone cortisol that passes through to their milk. When you drink cow's milk or consume other dairy products, you absorb their cortisol. As someone who is grieving, you have enough of your own cortisol! Do not add more by eating dairy products.

Milk can be a source of inflammation and, as mentioned earlier, when you are grieving it is important to reduce your inflammation. It is highly recommended to reduce or remove dairy from your diet.

Reduce Caffeine

You may turn to caffeine for energy. It can offer a short-term boost just like comfort foods, however, the letdown is more detrimental than the original so-called high. You may feel that you have to have another cup as you come down off the original surge. Your body can eventually crave this so much that you create an addiction to the energy boost.

Caffeine can also increase your blood pressure. It is quite common for a grieving parent to already be experiencing elevated blood pressure, and it is dangerous to artificially add to it with the use of stimulants from caffeine. Caffeine can also cause heart palpitations, and in turn, those can generate anxiety.

Caffeine also acts as a diuretic, which will increase your risk of dehydration. Remember, coffee, teas, and sodas do not count when hydrating your body. If you cannot absolutely survive without at least one cup of coffee, keep it to no more than one cup before 10:00 a.m.

Remember that a serving size of a single cup of coffee is eight to ten ounces. Be mindful if you are getting it from a coffee shop. These drinks are most probably much bigger than eight ounces, exceeding the recommended intake.

Reduce or Eliminate Alcohol

I recommend reducing or totally eliminating alcohol consumption while you are mourning. As previously mentioned in Chapter

5, alcohol can be a form of avoidance. A child's death by suicide is certainly one of the most upsetting and painful experiences you can experience in your lifetime. It is common to go through a wide range of emotions, from anger and denial to sadness and despair. Everyone goes through the grieving process differently, and some may not do it in the healthiest manner. You may turn to alcohol in an attempt to numb the sadness, pain, and grief that follows a major loss.

Sadly, self-medicating all that emotional pain often leads to alcohol addiction, even for the seemingly strongest and most resilient individuals. During the grieving process, it is critical that you experience and express emotions, so you can eventually move on with life and heal. However, some people get stuck as they begin struggling with unresolved grief.

There is no form of self-medicating with substances that will effectively erase the pain of loss. In fact, alcohol acts as a depressant in the body, intensifying emotions such as shame or sadness. Alcohol impairs every part of daily life, from the quality of relationships to the ability to hold down a job. Seriously consider removing alcohol from your diet for your physical and mental health.

Reduce Sugar and Eliminate Added Sugars

Sugar is found in many sources. It comes from processed foods and whole foods. Sugar is responsible for lack of energy, agitation, and weight gain, and it can weaken your immune system. Sugar is also responsible for mood swings, depression, and grief brain.

There are many types of sugar: dextrose, fructose, galactose, glucose, lactose, maltose, and sucrose. Sugar can be found in almost everything. You might be surprised to learn that these premade processed foods have added sugar: low-fat yogurt, chocolate milk, spaghetti sauce, barbecue sauce, sports drinks, granola, iced tea, protein bars, soups, breakfast cereal, smoothies, and salad dressing.

You might be sensing a theme here. Processed foods make you sick, increase your risk of multiple life-threatening diseases, and impair your ability to move through your grief.

You cannot totally eliminate sugar because it naturally occurs in the whole foods you eat. However, regardless of where the sugar comes from, there is a recommended daily allowance. The maximum consumption for women is 100 calories a day. This is twenty-five grams or six teaspoons of sugar.

A twenty-ounce bottle of Coca-Cola Classic contains sixty-five grams of sugar, which is forty grams above the daily recommended allowance. In other words, one bottle of Coke equates to about fifteen teaspoons of sugar! With just one bottle of Coke, you have exceeded the daily recommended allowance of sugar.

Sugar is now being noted as a greater contributor to heart disease than cholesterol. While I do not have empirical evidence that sugar contributes to broken heart syndrome, there is research that heart health is impacted by sugar. Going out on a limb, it is my logical conclusion that sugar can contribute to the risk and the signs and symptoms of broken heart syndrome.

I understand reducing your sugar intake may seem like an insurmountable task. However, reducing sugar will not only help with your health, but it will also help in your grief. Think twice before grabbing a soda, candy bar, or bag of chips.

Here are a few simple and easy healthy snacks:

- Apple and peanut butter
- Nuts: unsalted almonds, peanuts, cashews, walnuts
- Seeds: pepitas (pumpkin seeds), sunflower seeds, flaxseeds
- Plant-based protein smoothie
- Sliced carrots and celery with hummus
- Unsweetened plant-based yogurt with fresh fruit
- Hard-boiled egg
- Avocado toast (use gluten-free bread)
- Dark chocolate (limited quantity)
- Water with fruit

I have followed this healthy lifestyle before and after my son's death. It is an integral part of my overall health and healing from my loss. While there is no right or wrong way to grieve, there are healthy ways to cope with the pain.

Give yourself all the fighting power you can to help yourself move through your loss. You do not have to be perfect. Give yourself some grace. Take a few of these ideas every week and, in a few months, you will look back and see that you have focused on your health in the midst of your grief with more energy, less brain fog, and better sleep.

Sleep Hygiene

Sleep is the time when your body restores itself. This is when the brain goes on autopilot and the bodily functions slow down, allowing for repair and restoration. It is common for people to experience a change in their sleeping pattern in the days, weeks, and months following the loss of a loved one. You may have trouble falling asleep or staying asleep.

On the other end of the spectrum, grievers may find it difficult to stay awake. Their philosophy is that "when the going gets tough, the tough go to bed." Sleep becomes their only relief from their pain.

Here are some reasons why you might have difficulty sleeping after a loved one's death:

- Intrusive thoughts
- Worries and anxieties about stressors that have occurred as a result of the death of your child
- Bad dreams
- Disorders such as depression, insomnia, and posttraumatic stress disorder

If your lack of sleep seems marginal and you are dealing with more obvious and painful stressors, it's easy to overlook the impact fatigue might have on your emotional outlook. Unfortunately, if you are not cognizant of the importance of a good night's sleep, then you are far less likely to see it as necessary to healing in your grief journey.

The impact lack of sleep has is far reaching. Some of the consequences of little sleep are:

- Low tolerance for frustration
- Easily overwhelmed
- Irritability
- Anger
- Hostility
- Feeling more depressed
- Greater emotional reactivity

- Less friendly
- Less elated
- Less empathetic
- Negative
- Weaker immune response
- Hungrier and apt to eat more
- Weight gain

So how do you get better sleep? One of the things I like to focus on is sleep hygiene. You might be asking yourself, "What is she talking about?" Improving your sleep hygiene is an important piece of self-care and healing.

When I mention *sleep hygiene* most people look at me like I am crazy. This is a relatively new concept. Fifty years ago, as a society, we did not have the technology we have today. Television sets were being introduced to the home, but they stayed in the family room for family viewing and family time. Somehow, they moved into the bedroom and started disrupting many things including sleep.

Eventually other technology made its way into the bedroom: laptop computers, cell phones, tablets, smart speakers, blue-light clocks, security systems, and baby monitors.

The art of preparing oneself to go to bed and get a good night's sleep has been lost. The ritual of washing your face, brushing your teeth, and getting into jammies is a forgotten ritual. Instead, the TV blares nightly news of tragedy and devastation in the bedroom. Cell phones emit blue lights that stimulate your brain rather than allowing you to rest and relax. Text messages and other alerts ding all night long.

Do you scroll through social media at bedtime? Social media is a black sinkhole that draws you in and will not let you out. Add to this the fact that you are already in a place of grief and unrest; it is no wonder you have difficulty sleeping.

Improving your sleep hygiene is an important piece of self-care. Serotonin, the sleep hormone, increases with the more sleep you get. Getting quality sleep is a major step in helping your body to heal. It is during sleep that your physical body heals, and your brain relaxes. It is also one of the easiest forms of self-care if you decide to do it.

Follow these simple steps to improve your sleep hygiene:

- Remove the TV from your bedroom. The bedroom is a place for rest and relaxation not disaster stories or nasty political campaigns. The last things you hear before going to sleep is what is on your subconscious mind when you fall asleep, and negative thoughts are not what you want to feed your brain at bedtime. It is important to stop the use of technology and stop receiving the effects of the blue lights at least three hours before going to bed. Ensure your brain is not stimulated before trying to rest.
- Remove other electronics as well: laptop, tablet, and cell phone. If you are using electronics as your alarm, buy an old-fashioned alarm clock.
- Focus on washing your face and brushing your teeth before bedtime. Make it a habit again.
- Read a nonelectronic book. Complete your affirmations. Journal. Pray.

These suggestions may be a challenge for you. Start with something small. Remember why you want to improve your sleep and be deliberate in your actions. It will help with your grief journey.

Julie's Story

Julie is one of my former personal training clients. We lost touch over the years. Recently she was led to reach out to me. Initially it was for no other reason except to touch base during the pandemic. She told me her nephew took his life. She was close to him and was having a hard time with her loss. She was surprised to learn about Connor's death. It now made sense why she called me. It was not a coincidence. We were meant to connect and chat.

We talked about her nephew, what they liked to do when they were together, and what he was passionate about. She was grateful that I was available to listen, understand her journey, and bear witness to her loss. We transitioned to talking about her health.

During our training together, I taught Julie the value of taking care of herself. She knew in theory what to do now but had fallen off the path. Work took over, family obligations increased, complacency set in, and her grief sapped her energy. She was no longer taking care of herself.

When I asked Julie to recall how she had felt when she was exercising, getting sleep, eating well, and drinking water, her eyes lit up and a wide smile crossed her face. She told me she had felt great. Her attitude had been one of gratitude, and she had slept well. Oh, yes, those are the positive benefits of taking care of yourself.

I asked her if she thought this would apply in her current situation. She pondered for a moment and replied, "Yes, of course it does."

She was correct. All she needed to do was reestablish those routines. We agreed that I would be her accountability partner for the next thirty days. She would text me at the end of each day, reporting what she accomplished. Did she exercise? Did she eat well? Did she get the required sleep? Did she drink enough water? Did she complete her meditations?

After those thirty days, Julie was well on the path of consistency in taking care of herself. Now she was better equipped to process her nephew's passing, and she was also able to share her transformation with her nephew's mother, Gloria. Gloria saw there was hope to find joy and healing, and we are now working together to get her there.

Massage

In grief, massage is no longer a luxury, it becomes a necessity. Following a major loss, grief can move into your body, and you may find it difficult to release tension and stress on your own. Here are seven ways that massage can help in grief:

1. Massage can calm your nervous system.
2. Massage can release tension that causes headaches.
3. Massage can improve energy levels and your overall sense of wellbeing.
4. Massage can improve circulation.
5. Massage can reduce stress in your body.
6. Massage can allow you to mentally turn everything off.
7. Massage can help to flush out toxins, which accumulate in your lymph system as a result of grief.

After a massage, plan to take the remainder of the day off and rest. You may release emotions and toxins. This can be exhausting, mentally and physically. Be sure to drink extra water, above the recommended "one-half of your body weight (in ounces)" calculation presented earlier in this chapter. To maximize the massage effects, take a hot bath with Epsom salts. This will further get the toxins out.

The need to focus on becoming healthier can be immediate. It changes how you think and feel about your body. How much abuse can it withstand before breaking down? Without your health, you cannot move forward on your loss journey, let alone help someone else as discussed in Chapter 8's oxygen mask analogy. Consider exercise, sleep, water, and nutrition paths to make a positive change in your loss journey.

These are suggestions. There is no right or wrong. Do what feels right for you. Take what you like and leave the rest but do take something. You are here for a reason. You want to move forward in your grief journey. Self-care is an integral part of that journey.

Physical Health Summary

Unfortunately, physical health is a unique and foreign concept to many who are on a loss journey. I have spent a lot of time in this chapter discussing the tools that worked for me and providing examples of how they worked for my clients. Because this may be a new concept for you, I want to recap some key points about what I shared with you.

Physical health is an essential piece to move through your loss. It involves self-care and an activity, or activities, that you intentionally engage in to improve or regenerate your health. Grief takes a toll on your body; this is why it is necessary to include self-care in your recovery.

This chapter started by discussing exercise and how it produces endorphins that improve sleep and focus and reduce pain. There are a variety of methods to exercise. The three main types of exercise are cardiovascular, weight training, and stretching.

Within physical health is nutrition. It is common to stress-eat with so-called comfort foods in times of grief. While they provide relief, it is only short term and, in the long run, are detrimental to your recovery. Adding real food and plant-powdered Juice Plus+ capsules and drinking plenty of water are the first steps. Next, reduce or eliminate gluten and dairy. Finally, reduce caffeine, alcohol, and sugar. You will have more energy, sleep better, and have fewer digestion challenges. Ultimately this will give you room to focus on the other components of recovery: mental, emotional, and spiritual health.

Sleep hygiene is another component of self-care in grief. With sleep deprivation or poor-quality sleep irritability, overwhelm, and weight gain seem to prevail. Follow the simple steps of removing technology and stop using technology at least three hours before going to bed. Find other, relaxing activities that do not require technology.

Another form of self-care that loss travelers tend to forget is massage. In your grief, your body can experience aches and pains and increased levels of tension. Massage is a great way to refresh your body. It can also double as a way to refresh your mind. Nothing to do but relax and have the masseuse work out the tightness.

Remember, self-care is not selfish. It is part of your overall grief recovery.

"Take care of your body.
Your mental health will follow."
—Peggy Green

CHAPTER 15

PART 2: MENTAL HEALTH

Mental health is important throughout your grief journey, because it can help you to cope with the stresses of life, be physically healthy, and have good relationships. Did you know that physical health supports mental health, and mental health supports physical health? Mental health helps you make contributions to your community, work productively, and realize your full potential. It also helps to work through grief.

What Is Mental Health?

Allow me to offer a short definition. Mental health is your cognition, the beliefs, thoughts, and edicts you live by with peace of mind and happiness. Mental health encompasses the stories you tell yourself to make sure you survive and feel safe.

Grief is from the heart, but the stories come from your mind. Events and facts do not change. Death is death. Facts are exactly what happened without embellishment. However, the story you tell yourself can change. That is where you have some control. You are in charge of the way you think and the amount of pain you experience.

Your mind automatically kicks into survival mode when exposed to fear and danger. However, your conscious mind does not always do what is best for you. It can turn on you and talk you into thinking the worst-case scenarios.

Signs of Good Mental Health

During a coaching session, Eileen asked me for some examples of what someone with strong mental health looked like. I shared five signs of good mental health:

1. You feel good about yourself.
2. You do not become overwhelmed by emotions such as fear, anger, love, jealousy, guilt, or anxiety.
3. You have lasting and satisfying personal relationships.
4. You feel comfortable with other people and new situations.
5. You can laugh at yourself and with others.

Signs of Poor Mental Health

I also shared with her signs and symptoms of poor mental health. Poor mental health, also known as mental illness, refers to a wide range of conditions — disorders that affect your mood, thinking, and behavior. Based on my extensive research, I summarized the five basic categories of mental illness as:

1. Depression
2. Anxiety disorder
3. Addictive behaviors
4. Eating disorders
5. Schizophrenia

It is crucial to assess where you are currently in order to develop a plan of action. If you have mental illness, it is important to address this and open up space in your healing to grieve.

Mental illness is not to be taken lightly and should be diagnosed by a medical practitioner. If you feel you are experiencing symptoms of mental illness, please see your medical provider.

Mental health illnesses are not a normal part of the grieving process. You can survive the loss of a loved one without experiencing mental health symptoms. I will share more information on each of these mental health illnesses to help you identify if you may need to seek additional help.

Depression and Grief

Depression is unique when grieving. The loss of a loved one is different than the loss of a relationship or job. It is quite normal to feel sad. Frequently, as you go through loss, you may describe yourself as "depressed."

However, feeling sad is not the same as depression. Grieving is natural and shares some of the same features as depression, but depression is not a natural response to grieving. Both involve sadness and possible withdrawal from usual activities.

I believe this is how depression and grieving are different. Waves of sadness and pain will come and go with grief. With depression, losing interest in experiencing anything enjoyable will commonly last for several weeks or longer. Depression can pull you into an unescapable dark hole.

In grief, you may express the wish to "join" your loved one. In major depression, it is possible to focus on ending one's life due to feeling a lack of purpose, losing the desire to go on living, or feeling unable to cope with the pain of depression.

Grief and depression can co-exist. When grief is added to an already existing depression, the grief is more severe and may last longer than grief without depression.

Take a good, long look at your feelings. If you are questioning where you are, please see a licensed professional who can make a diagnosis.

Anxiety and Grief

The more you know about anxiety, the better off you are in working through it. Anxiety after loss is the result of being thrown into your own vulnerability, a place that is difficult to be. It can force you to confront your own mortality and other things you are not used to thinking about. Life becomes unpredictable, and this may raise anxiety levels.

What is anxiety? It comes from thoughts that may never occur. At its most elementary level, anxiety is the sense of fear. As you read in the chapters covering Phase II — Overcome Your Fear, your fears can be about something in the past, the present, or the future.

After the loss of a loved one, many things that you experience may feel like an even greater threat than before. After seeing someone die, death has now hit you squarely in the eyes. It is real and not something that only happens to other people. Your body and mind now have a stronger reaction to mortality than you did before this happened.

Signs and Symptoms of Anxiety

- Irregular heartbeat
- Dizziness and lightheadedness
- Shortness of breath
- Choking sensation and nausea
- Shaking and sweating
- Fatigue and weakness
- Chest pain and heartburn
- Muscle spasms
- Hot flashes or sudden chills
- Tingling sensations in your extremities
- A fear that you are going crazy
- A fear that you might die or be seriously ill

Anxiety is unique for everyone. Realize, though, that as you can see in the above list, it can manifest itself into very real physical symptoms. You can think there is something seriously physically wrong with you, while in reality it is your anxiety causing these reactions.

Grief plays tricks on you. As you learned earlier in this book, it can cause fear of letting go, fear of healing, fear of the unknown, fear of judgment, and the fear of losing someone else (death anxiety).

Understand that these are not the only types of fears and anxiety that exist.

Anxiety can occur when someone close to you dies. It is so important to allow yourself to grieve, so you can manage any anxiety that accompanies it. If you are questioning your levels of anxiety, please see a licensed professional who can make a diagnosis.

My Anxiety

This week I found myself crying and frustrated. The smallest things triggered me, from memories about a glass swan to the difficulty of taking a shower with a cast on my arm due to a recent auto accident, to having my son send me visions. This happened to me several times during the week. I even found I was procrastinating writing this week's *Thursday Thoughts*.

I spent some time in meditation to figure out what was causing all my frustration. It came to me in one word. *Anxiety.* Yes, even as a grief coach, I am human and feel emotions just like everyone else. However, my self-awareness guided me back to peace.

I got to work on myself and faced my anxiety head-on by journaling. I wrote about my son Connor. The last time I saw him was on a Thanksgiving holiday. We had a full house that day with friends and family. My daughters had invited their boyfriends and other friends were here to celebrate with us. The kids' father, whom I am no longer married to, joined us, and we had not spent a holiday together in years.

In the family "selfie" photo, my son has his left hand on my left shoulder. That is the last family picture with all three kids and both of their parents.

I bring this up, because in my journaling I realized that part of my anxiety is due to the upcoming holiday. A lot of things have changed, not just my son but the significant others. Life is different — there is both loss of life and loss of relationships. My anxiety is also being stimulated by my current loss of independence due to my auto accident.

With all that being said, the big realization is that I just do not have control over some things. As hard as I wish, I cannot bring my son back. I know that it is not possible, and the next time we meet will be in heaven. I miss him, and this will be another Thanksgiving without him. His memorial rock has been placed, and we are planning a dedication ceremony in December. I look forward to this celebration of Connor's life, as it is an added piece in closure.

My anxiety has now lifted, and I am grateful that it has passed. Through the years I have gained multiple ways to help myself in difficult times with the use of various tools such as journaling.

The good news, anxiety is treatable! Keep doing your work.

Addictive Behaviors and Grief

Grief and trauma are two of the most common underlying causes of addiction. Emotions experienced in grief can make simple day-to-day activities difficult to manage. Grieving takes time to navigate emotions of denial, sadness, anger, and more. While on this journey, you are reforming neural pathways in your brain. Mood-altering substances halt the process, and your brain is unable to move past the healing stage it was in when the substance was first introduced.

An example will help. If a loved one started drinking heavily at age twenty-one years old, then their brain maturity will not move past that age, even though their physical body ages. Mood-altering substances stall the maturation process, which delays or even postpones the grieving process.

As you are aware, grief can be overwhelming. It is your response to the death of a loved one — your child. Humans are taught to avoid pain, and everyone deals with it differently. Some cry, some become angry, and others turn to drugs or alcohol.

There is no right way to feel, and everyone walks through the grieving process in their own way. However, there is a healthy way to grieve, and substance abuse is not one of them. For those who already meet criteria for a substance-use disorder, the loss — or more specifically, the inability to process the loss — only compounds the underlying issues.

Using drugs and alcohol will not take away your pain. They can temporarily numb you. However, drug and alcohol use have consequences. Alcohol is a depressant and can make you feel worse after you use it. When drugs or alcohol are used to help numb the emotions, excessive use can lead to addiction.

When someone close to you dies there is a possibility that you will try to replace that person or relationship with something else. Feeling empty and knowing you will never see, speak to, or hear from someone you love ever again can be devastating, leading to running away from the pain with drugs and alcohol.

Using drugs and alcohol are not necessary to cope with the loss of a loved one. They do not have to be the end solution. Alcohol and drugs only provide momentarily relief, and their risks are far greater than the benefits.

If these words describe your situation, seek help in addition to your grief healing.

Eating Disorders and Grief

As a result of grief, an eating disorder can develop when your ability to cope is low. You can often struggle to cope and adapt to life changes when grieving. Focusing on food and your body can become an easy target in which you seek comfort or distraction through certain behaviors. This is similar to drug and alcohol addiction.

While some initial appetite changes are often normal when grieving, prolonged reliance and focus on food or weight to cope can quickly lead to an eating disorder.

To determine if this describes your situation, consider the following symptoms. Are you experiencing one or more of these symptoms of eating disorder?

- Severe fluctuations in weight
- Loss of appetite that leads to purposeful limited caloric intake
- Incidents of binge eating
- Purging behaviors (vomiting, laxative use, diuretic use, excessive exercise)
- Fixation with numbers including calorie counting, weight, and clothing size
- Decreased socialization to avoid food-related activities

The impact of grief is wide and varies from physiological to emotional changes. Stress hormone levels rise. As a defense, your body may go into "survival mode" and begin taking protective measures. Blood is shoved to the arms and legs and away from the gut. Cortisol levels increase, suppressing hunger and appetite.

SURVIVE YOUR CHILD'S SUICIDE

Anxiety and panic can even surface as aversions to foods or textures. Some people in grief experience nausea and vomiting. This can make caring for the body's nutritional needs exceedingly difficult.

As serotonin (the happy, calm chemical) levels fall, you may be drawn to sugars and carbs for a pick-me-up. You may try to use food to comfort the emotional pain associated with grief and loss. Sleep disruptions may develop, further draining your body of vital energy. A sleep-deprived, physically exhausted, and emotionally depleted body may look for extra food to nourish it even though what it desperately needs is rest, recovery, and healing. Bottom line, feeding yourself during the grief process may be fraught with complications.

You can cope with these complications by being armed with the self-care skills discussed in the previous chapter on physical health.

I highly recommend you eat breakfast to encourage your body to want and need nutrition. Something healthy such as a piece of fruit, a protein shake, or a handful of nuts are good simple alternatives.

A profound loss can naturally disrupt the rhythm of eating, and you need to make space for this process. Proper nutrition is crucial while you grieve, so if you feel that eating has become unmanageable, do not hesitate to ask for help. You are not alone.

Schizophrenia and Grief

Grief does not cause schizophrenia, but it can impact an existing condition. In exceedingly rare cases, grief can cause psychosis or the development of psychotic symptoms.

Schizophrenia is a serious mental disorder in which people interpret reality abnormally. Schizophrenia may present as some combination of hallucinations, delusions, extremely disordered thinking, and behavior that impairs daily functioning, which can be disabling.

Researchers in this field are finding that the death of a loved one contributes to the change of neuropathways, which may trigger schizophrenia. If you believe you are experiencing a serious mental disorder, please seek professional help immediately.

The following pages present tools that can help you strengthen and improve your mental health.

Use Words to Improve Your Mental Health

Because you have experienced loss, you have the ability to feel deeper in the darker emotions of pain and suffering and the lighter ones of peace and joy.

It is easier for your brain to recall the dark emotions because it has a natural tendency to give weight to (and remember) negative experiences or interactions more than positive ones — they stand out more.

Therefore, it is important now more than ever to choose your words wisely and bring out the good. Because what you tell yourself is fundamental to processing, growing through grief, and finding meaning.

"Change your story, change your life."
—Peggy Green

Pursue Personal Growth

Personal growth is just that. You decide what area in your life you would like to develop. Is there a hobby you would like to learn? Is there an organization where you can volunteer on behalf of your child? You have options. It may take several attempts until you find one that helps. You can make a list of the areas you want to grow in, master the activity, mark it off, then move onto the next item. Personal growth takes the focus off your grief and channels your energy toward positive outcomes.

Personal growth can scare the people around you. They may discourage you from becoming a better person. They like you as you are, even if you want to improve. They may question why you want to do so because of their insecurities of losing the person they are familiar with as you grow and change.

As for yourself, you may possibly deny the opportunity to grow. Maybe you tried before and gave up before seeing results. Being prideful may stop you from seeing that personal growth can help with your grief. One of the largest obstacles is negative self-talk and not believing that you can expand in a variety of new, exciting, and healthy ways.

Use Questions to Improve Your Mental Health

Every day you ask yourself questions and automatically, without much thought, you respond. "Should I wear the white blouse or the print one? Should I have bacon or sausage with my eggs? Should I take route A to work or route B?" These are small, inconsequential questions. In answering these questions, you will have a different experience. The answers do not impact the way you see yourself.

Now look at what you tell yourself — and how the questions you ask yourself can change your thinking and your future. For example, have you told yourself that you will never, ever get over the death of your child? If that is what you tell yourself, then you will not get over it. First, you do not "get over" a loss. You move through your grief to healing.

Second, if you were to change this statement to a question that brought about good thoughts, how would this make you feel? Ask yourself:

- Am I open to healing?
- What does it look like to move forward?
- How would changing the way I look at my loss impact my future?
- What do I want to change about my thoughts?

Asking yourself these questions with a good, positive outlook will change the neuropathways in your brain. You will create fresh paths for your thoughts to follow — good new thoughts. Eventually, those old, worn paths will stop being used, and you will have formed new ways of thinking.

It takes a considerable amount of energy to think, whether your thoughts are positive or negative. Instead of negative thoughts that are detrimental to your progress in your grief journey, consider putting your energy toward positive thoughts that help you move to healing. This takes some practice and effort. I know you can do it.

Unplug from Social Media

There are so many uses for social media. Businesses use it for communication, collaboration, and reviews of products and services. Consumers use it for entertainment, news, and connection.

However, with easy access, twenty-four-hour availability, and new programs being introduced every few months, it is easy to get drawn into the black hole of being overinformed, making comparisons with other people's lives, and taking in unhealthy amounts of negativity.

These past few years have been quite challenging with the COVID-19 pandemic, polarization of politics, a heightened focus on racial injustice, new wars and conflicts erupting, and so much more. Personally, you may have lost a job, lost your home, or experienced the loss of a loved one. The list goes on and on.

It is quite likely that, in this season of your life, you turned to social media. It is easy to get caught up in the play-by-play information of disturbing news and endless postings. It can overtake your thoughts, shift your mood, and change your attitude. You can disconnect from the real world and lose all track of time — a convenient form of escapism.

After scrolling through social media, do you feel more stressed than normal? Does your anxiety level rise? Do you feel lonely in spite of being "connected" to others through social media? That's because social media is actually a form of isolation.

It is possible you need to unplug from social media! Think about how you handled stress and anxiety before the introduction of social media. Maybe you called someone who would empathetically listen, hearing the tension in your voice and telling you that you would be okay. Through conversation, you possibly came up with a solution to your problem. Did you have family dinners together where you could look someone in the eyes and ask how their day was? Dinner is a time to connect over food, be grateful, and rejoice.

Do not get me wrong, social media has its good points. In grief, social media can be a platform to receive support from a larger group from those experiencing a similar loss. It is the overuse, addiction, and life-altering consequences that are so wrong.

To improve your mental health relationships and reduce anxiety and stress, I suggest you briefly unplug from social media every week. I have been making it a practice to unplug from 5:00 p.m. Saturday to 5:00 p.m. Sunday every week.

I know I am okay without it, and the world will do just fine without me commenting on other people's lives. If I miss something that is super important in those twenty-four hours, I am counting on a friend or family member to pick up the phone and call me.

The tools you are learning in this book will help you move forward in your healing journey. Remember to pull them out and use them frequently. The more often you use them, the more second nature they become.

CHAPTER 16

PART 3: EMOTIONAL HEALTH

Emotional health is one aspect of *mental health*. I am focusing on emotional health, because the tools I offer are different than those I recommend for mental health.

Having good emotional health is a fundamental aspect of fostering resilience, self-awareness, and overall contentment. This is something that you may struggle with since losing your loved one. Good emotional health is your ability to cope with both positive and negative emotions, which includes your awareness of them. Good emotional health is the soul's barometer for navigating the feel-bad emotions when life gets tough.

I want to really stress that there are no positive or negative emotions. There are only feel-good or feel-bad emotions. Think of it this way, if you say being happy is a positive emotion, you judge yourself as experiencing an "acceptable" emotion. If you say crying is a negative emotion, then you can associate it with doing something wrong. When you think it is wrong to cry, then you discount your grief. You tell yourself, "Crying is wrong, therefore, I should not be doing it."

Good emotional health does not always mean being happy. It does mean you are aware of your emotions and can determine if you feel good or feel bad. Emotionally healthy people still experience stress, anger, and sadness. The difference is you know how to navigate these emotions either on our own or with a professional like myself.

Emotional health also affects your physical health. Research shows a link between an upbeat mental state and physical signs of good health. These include lower blood pressure, reduced risk of heart disease, and a healthier weight.

Why Seek Good Emotional Health in Grief?

Working on your emotional health is just as important as taking care of your physical wellbeing. Improving your emotional health pays off with a greater resilience to stress. Stress caused by grief can make you more vulnerable to physical illness, weakening your immune system. As a result, you may start to notice you are getting sick more frequently with greater intensity. As you are aware, losing a loved one to suicide is stressful enough, and you do not want to add getting sick to your stressors.

In grief, it is common to have different grieving styles versus those around you. The better you are equipped to handle your emotions, the easier it will be to maintain your relationships. You can show more empathy and compassion for others. An added bonus it that you are less likely to argue, instead being able to talk through your feelings.

As I have mentioned, grief can leave you feeling guilty and responsible for your child's death. It can leave you feeling bad about yourself. Having the skills to navigate your grief will open the door for higher self-esteem and the ability to see the best in yourself, despite your loss.

When you are emotionally depleted, it tends to also deplete you physically. Remember that all four areas of your health are related to moving through your grief: physical, mental, emotional, and spiritual. A positive outlook will help you to feel lighter and help to lift the weight off your shoulders. It takes practice and repeated efforts **to work on your emotional health.**

Signs and Symptoms of Good Emotional Health

It is helpful to see what both good and poor emotional health looks like. By no means is the following list all encompassing. It is a place to start, to look inward and see if you need additional help. This list might be the catalyst to propel you forward and seek other resources.

People who are emotionally healthy:

- Are in control of their thoughts, feelings, and behaviors
- Are able to cope with life's challenges
- Can keep problems in perspective and bounce back from setbacks
- Feel good about themselves
- Have good relationships

Signs and Symptoms of Poor Emotional Health

Examples of what poor emotional health looks like:

- Consistent feelings of sadness or hopelessness
- More than usual irritability, anger, aggression, or hostility
- Prolonged tearfulness or frequent crying
- Withdrawal from friends and family
- Loss of interest in activities you used to love
- Changes in eating and sleeping habits
- Unusual restlessness and agitation

Wait to Make Major Life Decisions

As you are well aware, the death of a child ranks as one of the most stressful life events. Given the toll grief can have on your emotional and physical health, I highly recommend that you delay any critical life decisions.

If you are thinking about selling your home or moving, consider delaying this for at least six months. Moving is another life stressor. It may be tempting to escape reminders of your loved one, however, you may also be escaping memories that will eventually turn into good ones. That is not an added burden to place on yourself.

Returning to a work environment that does not understand death and grief can also be stressful. You may be tempted to leave your job or change careers. In your grief, recognize that you are more sensitive and, most likely, not thinking clearly and normally. Things that were said or done that did not bother you before your loss can be magnified and appear more offensive. Those who are trying to help may not know how or simply bumble over what they do say.

Give yourself time before submitting your resignation. You will not feel like you do now forever. You will learn how to cope with your loss at home and at work.

Carol and the Three C's

I am thankful that I get to help grieving moms. Just last week I was working with Carol, who lost a child four months ago. She was experiencing guilt since her daughter took her life. Carol told me she could never, ever release herself of the guilt. She was not sleeping and had a lot of anxiety as a result.

When she first started working with me, she was afraid of being judged by others. She felt others blamed her for everything, and she did not deserve to do anything but feel guilty.

I shared the three C's with her.

1. You cannot *control* others.
2. You cannot *cure* other people's problems.
3. You did not *cause* them to do what they did.

Even though she wanted to take on responsibility I revoked her superpower to *control* others. She looked at me as if I were speaking a foreign language. She had always thought she was responsible for missing the signs and symptoms of her daughter's emotional state before she died.

Carol also felt she failed her daughter and did not protect her, even though she did everything she could with the information she had at the time. She thought she could *cure* her problems. I revoked that superpower as well.

Carol thought she caused her daughter to take her life, because the night before she died, they had an argument. Carol did not *cause* her daughter to do anything. Her daughter freely made her decision.

Once Carol was able to realize that she did not control, cure, or cause what her daughter did, she was able to release herself of feeling guilty for her daughter's suicide. Carol is now giving herself permission to release her guilt. She understands that others do not blame her for anything. She did not control, cure, or cause her daughter to end her life.

Addressing your emotions and feelings does not happen overnight. It takes a shift in your mindset about your circumstances. Let us talk about this for a few minutes.

Mindset

Mindset is a collection of thought patterns and beliefs that shape your view of reality. It is a story you tell yourself about your identity and about the world around you. Changing your mindset is one of the most beneficial things you can do to help deal with your emotions. It is also one of the hardest.

You have probably heard the saying, "mind over matter." This refers to one's ability to use conscious and subconscious thoughts over physical limitations. Remember, your subconscious thoughts control your mind more than you may know. When you are mindful, you can control your emotions and feelings by changing your subconscious thoughts.

Do you tell yourself that you do not know how to overcome your loss? You could be telling yourself that you do not deserve happiness, that you are responsible for your child's passing, or even that you cannot live without them, now or ever. You may be saying this to yourself, someone else may be telling you, or it can be a combination of the two. These thoughts burn into your subconscious mind. It is no wonder you might be having difficulty working through your emotions when there are untruths guiding every thought you have.

The more you think the same thoughts over and over, the more ingrained they become into your mindset. These thoughts literally form pathways in your brain by connecting neurons over and over again. It is like a well-worn path through a field. If you walk the same path over and over, you will wear down the grass. The same thing happens in your brain as you reinforce certain neural pathways through repeated thoughts.

Your thought patterns are meant to protect you from harm. Your mind is exceptionally good at doing that. It keeps you from experiencing pain, even though pain is necessary to move through your grief.

Changing your mindset and subconscious thoughts are difficult to work through. You must be vulnerable to the possibility of pain and willing to walk through it to heal. It takes time and work to uncover what your subconscious mind is telling you and then shift the messages. Your subconscious mind has immense power in controlling your life experiences — your response to grief, anger, guilt, and sadness.

Grief Affirmations

You have taken a good look at the way you think about your circumstances and situation. It is time to learn how to think differently about them. Using affirmations is a simple and easy way to modify your thinking patterns.

Grief affirmations can be said anytime and anywhere. They are a great pick-me-up. No need to memorize them. You can write them on index cards and carry them with you. Having two sets is convenient, with one set at home and the other in your purse so it is always handy.

While saying affirmations does change what you believe and ultimately changes your conscious thoughts and actions, rewiring your brain takes time, effort, and guidance. Affirmations must be written very specifically because, if written incorrectly, they could do more harm than good. It is a good idea to work with someone such as myself, who is experienced in writing effective affirmations.

Affirmations rewire your thoughts. They are said in the present tense. Saying them in the present tense works with the subconscious mind. When you solely rely on the conscious mind to make a change, it prevents you from moving forward. It is those inner thoughts that drive your decisions and changing those is a great place to start. Affirmations bring related mental images into the mind, which inspire, energize, and motivate.

I have ten affirmations I do every single day. I do them in the morning with my cup of tea and before I go to sleep at night. If I miss saying them in the morning, I feel like I woke up on the wrong side of the bed. They set the stage for the way I think throughout the day and are the positive thoughts I go to sleep with every night.

My favorite affirmation is "I am a great mother and always will be." Here are some affirmations you may find useful.

Fourteen Grief Affirmations to Deal with Loss

1. *The pain in my heart is healing.* — The pain in your heart will heal in time. Remind yourself of this throughout the day each day. The void left behind when someone you love dies can feel as if it's always going to be there. There may be a part of you that dies when you suffer any type of significant loss, but your heart will mend. Your rational mind will never understand what has happened, but if you keep your heart open, it will find its way to healing. Trust the process.

2. *I have changed as a result of my grief.* — With the death of a loved one comes significant change. Your role at home and work will change as does your identity. Some people may tell you that things will resume as they were. The reality is that you will need to live with a new normal. Things will no longer be the same. You will become a different person. Hold on to the thought that, regardless of loss, you are not the same person today as you were yesterday.

3. *My love for (your loved one's name) lives forever.* — Love does not end when physical life ceases. You will not forget what it felt like to receive their love. You may decide to continue celebrations and special days even after their death to show how much they were loved and still are loved.

4. *I let go of my grief* — This reminds you that you do not have to wallow in your grief. You know when the right time is to let go of your suffering. While letting go of your grief, you can hold on to love. Be prepared that the pain may ebb and flow and that you may need to let go of your grief multiple times.

5. *Today is a good day for healing.* — Every day that you survive takes you one step closer from grief to healing. Start your day off with this affirmation, wiring positivity into your thoughts for the rest of the day.

6. *I am blessed.* — Thinking of how blessed you are when a loved one has died is more than likely a difficult concept to grasp. However, when you focus on what you have and think of the positive things you had prior to your loss, it becomes easier to believe.

7. *(Your loved one's name) has completed the circle of life.* — The circle of life is a concept that life comes to an end, and a truth that has been around since the beginning of time. You understand it, but when it happens to you it is a shock. You allow grief and sorrow to overtake your understanding of life and death. This affirmation reminds you that everything will cease to exist one day.

8. *My life has meaning.* — You were born with a meaning and purpose in mind. I know this to be true. While I do not like the circumstances I have been dealt, I now have a greater purpose to live than before. I am here to honor my son by helping other mothers move through physical, mental, emotional, and spiritual suffering caused by child suicide and live a meaningful and purposeful life. It is important to cherish the memories you have. They will last a lifetime.

9. *I am supported in my grief.* — At times you may feel you are not supported. Remember you have your higher power to call upon, friends who are willing to help you, and support groups that are available as well as grief coaches

and therapists. You do not need to walk this journey alone. If you are alone, it is a decision you are making.

10. *I am alive in my grief.* — Pain reminds you that you are a living, breathing human who experiences pain and sadness. Suffering from loss is part of your humanity.

11. *I choose love. I choose to heal.* — In your grief, you decide how you feel. Choosing love will guide you to a place of healing.

12. *I forgive my loved one for dying.* — You may be angry that your child died before you, especially if they died by their own hand, and you may find it difficult to forgive them. Forgiveness is not about them; it is about you being able to release your anger.

13. *I give myself permission to grieve.* — You may find yourself in situations where a grief wave strikes, and you want to run away. While this may seem the best possible solution, you are taking away an opportunity to process the pain and move forward in your healing. You may want to give yourself permission to grieve when and where it surfaces. You may feel that others are watching and judging, but does it really matter?

14. *I give myself permission to heal.* — You are allowed to rebuild your life. Your deceased child is not going to be angry with you. As a matter of fact, they most likely would be encouraging you to move forward.

For additional grief affirmations, please see Appendix 3.

Music for Healing

Driving seems to be the time that my grief surfaces. I think it is because that is when I received the phone call that my son killed himself.

Now, most days, I drive in silence. News is turned off, Siri is shut down, and podcasts are put on hold. I've learned to appreciate the quietness and solitude. This is a form of meditation in which I enjoy the scenery and allow thoughts to come in that otherwise would be shut out by all the incoming information competing for my attention.

I ask God to reveal to me who to pray for. Last week, I prayed for everyone who has cancer or is related to someone who is sick with cancer. I also asked for ways to continue to heal my heart, take away the pain, and move forward in my grief. The answer that came to me was music. However, sometimes God's answers are not clear, so I started a quest to gain clarity.

I looked into different genres — including my son's playlists — and ended up with a long list. Each song has different words that lift me up. Some offer the truth, in a gentle way, that the death of a loved one is tough, yet the reality is that life goes on.

Other songs spoke about acceptance when they are gone because of suicide. These songs really caught my attention. I felt the songwriter's pain. I knew their suffering. I felt a connection. I knew an artist would not write and sing a song on such an intense subject without personal experience. I felt as if we knew each other, even though we never met.

I heard gratitude for the loved one who was gone. Although their time on earth was cut too short, the time they were here is fondly remembered. I felt empathy flowing through the words and music.

I was comforted by songs that gave me hope to see my son again. I envisioned the angels looking down on me. Another singer crooned of the splendor of heaven. It allowed me to believe that my son is in a beautiful place, surrounded by goodness.

I listened to Connor's playlist, because I wanted insight to his personal taste in music. I got an earful. I quickly skipped songs I did not care for. There were some from his collection that I enjoyed, and I added them to my playlist. I became excited when I remembered listening to many of them with my son. There were Christian songs, which leads me to believe that he indeed did believe in God. That in itself makes my heart sing! One of his songs even talks about dancing and singing in heaven. That I took to heart. That is my Connor, and I am at peace.

Music — all different genres and varying messages — can help to heal your soul. It is just one more resource to add to your toolbox when you need a little extra help on your grief journey.

CHAPTER 17

PART 4: SPIRITUAL HEALTH

S piritual health is a personal matter involving values, integrity, and compassion and supports the purpose and mission of your life. It is better to ponder the meaning of life for yourself and to be accepting of the beliefs of others than to close your mind and become intolerant.

Spiritual wellness provides you with systems of faith, beliefs, values, ethics, principles, and morals. A healthy spiritual practice may include volunteerism, social contributions, belonging to a group, fellowship, optimism, forgiveness, and expressions of compassion and gratefulness.

Gratitude in Grief

As someone who is grieving you may find it difficult to be grateful. However, gratitude has the power to help you rise above your loss. It is life-affirming and can provide hope and healing in your darkest hour.

Turn your grief into gratitude. Focusing on gratitude helps to let go of the past pain and focus on the positive that surrounds you. In your grief, it may be difficult to feel an ounce of gratitude. You might even ask why you should be grateful for anything, especially in the wake of the death of your child. It seems unfathomable!

It is here that you trust the process, lean into those who have gone through it, and look at where they are now. Gratitude allows you to move through your profound pain and suffering. Your grief will shift, so you can learn to live with your loss.

Gratitude offers a blueprint to feeling joy again. It heals. It is a tool for coping with grief, especially during the holidays. Expressing gratitude does not need to be complicated. You can do it with any of the following suggestions. Do all of them, or at least do some of them. Doing nothing will keep you trapped in your darkest hour that turns into days, weeks, months, and years.

- Daily write down three things you are grateful for. Somedays it might be as simple as a hot shower.
- Verbally express gratitude with phrases such as:
  - You are the best.
  - I cannot say thank you enough.
  - How kind of you.
  - You've been helpful.
  - I want to say thank you for all your support and concern.
- Volunteer your time to an organization in honor of your loved one.

- Do an act of kindness. Pay for someone's coffee. Open a door.
- Donate to charity.
- Write a letter of appreciation.

Ultimately, showing gratitude can make you more optimistic. Research shows it decreases stress and improves physical and mental health with the production of feel-good hormones. You have the power within you to deal with your grief. Gratitude is acceptance while embracing the fact that you are in a new chapter of life.

To Believe or Not to Believe

A higher power is a supreme deity or other conception of God. Maybe you do not believe in God but do believe there is something bigger than you. It is what you turn to that explains the unexplainable. Your higher power is what gives you peace and rest. I believe in God and will refer to Him as such throughout this chapter. If that is not your belief, feel free to insert "higher power" when I describe God.

I have seen it happen time and time again. The loss of a loved one changes a person. It changes your inner being, who you are, and what you believe. If you once believed in God, you may now be screaming out in anger asking, "Why?" You may question how a loving God could allow this to happen. The pain is so great and the understanding so difficult that all faith in God may be lost. You may have been a devout Christian with an unshakeable relationship with God, but now you could be dismissing your faith at the mention of His name.

Or you may not have had any sort of faith in God but are now drawn to Him in this difficult time. A grieving mother may not have anywhere else to turn. God is their last resort in their suffering. They may have come to terms that they cannot survive the suicide of their child without a supreme being that gives them strength and courage.

After my son died, I changed from being a "holiday" church attender and believer to a daily meditator, prayer warrior, and believer who looks for God to show Himself. It is absolutely amazing what happens when God is on my radar and how He reveals what I am supposed to see. He shows me only what is relevant. God has given me comfort in knowing He is the Almighty Healer. It is through Him that I have hope, peace, and joy. I invite you to explore the possibilities.

Essentially the values that most humans live by are being good people, kind, and caring — all of the things that as a Christian you strive for. I saw this acronym, which I feel is a good place to start if you do not believe in God:

G — GOOD

O — ORDERLY

D — DIRECTION

How a Higher Power Can Help in Your Grief

I was one of those kids who occasionally went to church with my mom. I attended a Lutheran church and went through confirmation, but it never carried into my adulthood. However, I did get married in a church, just because it was the thing to do. I did not have a connection with God. After the death of my first child, both my mom and sister invited me to church and encouraged me to find God on a personal level. At the time, I was not ready to take the steps to move forward.

God revealed Himself to me when I was in a dark time and was not expecting Him to show Himself. I started attending Al-Anon, which is a twelve-step program for friends and family of alcoholics. It was a huge resource for me while I was living with my alcoholic then-husband. This was about the same time my dad was diagnosed with cancer. One of the principles of Al-Anon is to find your higher power. That is what finally got me back to church. I used my father's dying as an excuse to get my kids to church. It was a cover for me to teach them about God, and it was a place for me to seek support while living with an alcoholic. I went back to church for all the wrong reasons.

When my son got big enough that I could not physically carry him to the car, he decided to stop attending church. His dad did not support me taking him to church, so it was a tough battle that I lost. However, Connor did come to seek a higher power through the twelve-step programs he attended as an adult. He sometimes called the outdoors his higher power. It guided and directed him. I prayed that he would come to God someday. I was unsure if he believed in God or not.

As I mentioned, after his death I found some Christian songs on his playlist. Songs about God and believing in more than the outdoors as his higher power. When I heard those songs, I knew that without a doubt he believed in God. I cannot express how happy I am to know that.

Wherever you are in your relationship with God, give Him some time to speak to you. God heals all wounds. He gives you the strength to pick yourself up. I relate to God and cannot imagine being on this journey without Him. Surrender to God. Let Him help you. Let

Him guide you. Let Him love you in a time when it is challenging to love yourself.

The Bible is packed with people being real with God about their circumstances, expressing a whole range of emotions. God will offer you peace and comfort in your time of grief. He loves you and knows that you are suffering.

The writer of Psalm 22 cries out, "My God, my God, why have you forsaken me?" (v. 1). Job, who loses everything, does not hold back his grief. He and the psalmists help to find words for your own experience, or even to accept that there often are no words (Job 2:13). It is not always pretty, but God comes close to those who bring their grief to Him rather than suppress it.

God is not immune or indifferent to grief; He has experienced it at the deepest level possible with the death of His son Jesus Christ. And this same God is with you in your grief. He does not always tell you why you are suffering, but He does offer himself: "The Father of all compassion and the God of all comfort, who comforts us in all our troubles" (Cor 1:3-4).

If God does not exist, this is the only life we get. Death marks the end, and the loss is permanent. But if He does exist, then death does not have the last word. Jesus has defeated it. And one day, He will remove it entirely. On that day, God will personally wipe away all your tears and bury your grief for good. There is hope.

Salvation

Scripture teaches that, from the moment we truly believe in Christ, we are guaranteed eternal life. Christians know they have eternal life because it is stated in the Bible. God created mankind and those who are Christians will not be separated from God.

The myth that suicide is a deterrent to entrance into heaven is incorrect. Rather it is whether they are saved or unsaved. As the person dies, it is entirely possible that they have a last-second change of heart, crying out for God's mercy. We are not privileged to have that answer. It is a judgment that comes from God.

Believers can and do struggle with despair. According to the Bible, suicide is murder. Murder, as a sin, comes from the devil.

Yet, God is merciful. He forgives our sins. Jesus Christ died on the cross for our sins, even if they happen at the time of death. In other words, if you believe that Christ's sacrifice covers every sin, the sin of taking one's own life is no different than any other sin. Horrific and heartbreaking, yes — but not unforgivable.

Messages from God

Over 300 people attended my son's memorial service. The majority of those who attended were from school and numerous twelve-step programs he was involved with. The pastor who conducted the service shared with me his intuition that many of those who came were nonbelievers. In fact, he felt a sense of hatred toward God.

During Connor's service the pastor wanted to give his friends and family a way to understand that God was not responsible for my son's death. He wanted to let them know that God was with him in his final moments, that God would not just allow my son to end his life. God was standing next to him, screaming in his ear, "Don't do it. Don't do it. Don't do it." God could have stopped him, but He did not. He let Connor follow his free will. That is one of the biggest realizations that has helped me to move through my grief. God did not kill my son. He killed himself. God is with me in my grief.

Another powerful message came from a chaplain I worked with in my personal grief recovery. We talked about my son taking his life. What was going through his head and what he was experiencing had to be so bad that he felt ending it all was the only way out. The pain must have been unbearable. The chaplain shared with me that whatever demons were haunting him were now gone. They were no longer sitting on Connor's shoulders and weighing him down. Satan no longer has a hold on him. God now has my son in His arms.

Stop Accepting Your Circumstances

A friend, Claire, and I recently had dinner together. We have been friends for a few years. However, in the time we have known each other, she never revealed to me her anger that her brother died by suicide when he was in his mid-twenties. He was a few year older than her, and they were very close. She admitted she carried that anger every day, every moment of her life. She felt like something was wrong with her. She rarely spent time with friends and did not recognize who she was.

As a matter of fact, our planned dinners had been cancelled and rescheduled multiple times, always with her telling me she was tired and not feeling well. I always accepted what she said, because she was working full-time with two young children. Now the truth was revealed.

As our conversations progressed, in addition to her anger, Claire told me she was depressed, lacked energy, and wanted to curl up on the couch and stay there. She was listless at her job, doing the bare minimum to keep her job, let alone excelling to receive the much-needed performance-based raise.

Her children were in sports. She dropped them off at practice and instead of staying to cheer them on and chat with the other moms on the sidelines, she went to her car and slept, setting an alarm to ensure she was awake before her child came running to the car when the game or practice was over.

Claire admitted she was angry at her brother and still had not moved forward in her grief. She felt like she never grieved his death, and the pain is as raw now as the day he died. She could not talk about him. The guilt over feeling like she could have done something, anything, to stop him was like a dark, ominous rain cloud ready to burst. Shame of how he died, suicide, took her away from her faith. She had heard suicide was a sin and that hurt. She was afraid her brother did not make it to heaven.

I care deeply for this woman. She is a friend and a Sister in Christ. I felt called to share with her something I heard the previous week in church. I know it helped me immensely.

The pastor shared that he experiences anxiety and depression and said it is time to start fighting back. It is time to stop blaming yourself. It is time to stop accepting your depression. It is time to start your march toward freedom, from grief to healing. You do not need to stay in this place.

It is time to step up and fight the enemy. But who is the enemy? It is not anxiety. It is not depression. It is not grief. The enemy is the evil one who twists what was intended for good into something bad. He twists the fact that you are a survivor and tells you that you are depressed. He twists God's promises of hope, peace, and joy into desperation and depression.

God tells us that we were created with a fighter spirit, and it is time to tap into it. He has given you the weapons and His promises. One of His many promises: Romans 15:13: "May the God of Hope fill you with all joy and peace as your trust in Him, so that you may overflow with hope by the power of the Holy Spirit."

God gives that fighting spirit through positivity, mindset, and prayer. He wants you to take the first step into battle yet assuring you that He is by your side. He will fight the battle; you need to be willing to go to battle. When you are at your weakest, He is at His strongest.

If you cannot imagine healing, God will do it. If you cannot imagine hope. God will bring it to you. If you cannot imagine peace, God will show you. Do not let your hopelessness be debilitating.

One of my favorite versus that keeps my eyes focused on walking through my battles is Jeremiah 29:1, "'For I know the plans I have for you,' declares the Lord, 'plans to prosper you and not to harm you, plans to give you hope and a future. Then you will call upon me and come and pray to me, and I will listen to you. You will seek me and find me when you seek me with all your heart.'"

Remember, you do not have to stay in your circumstances. Stop accepting depression and anger. Step into the warrior that you are.

Use Prayer to Fight the Enemy

I find that praying is an opportunity to talk with God, tell Him what is on my mind, and ask for help. Prayer is easy to do and can be as simple as saying the word "help." The Holy Spirit knows what is on your heart, so even thinking a prayer counts. The Holy Spirit intercedes on your behalf and helps God to see your heart. Prayers do not have to be perfect. We can pray to God because Jesus took away that barrier, and we have full access to the Father. Unlike our earthly fathers, God does not get mad when we are angry with Him. Instead, He draws us closer.

Prayers can be said anywhere and anytime. There is no judgment. In fact, God wants us to talk to Him all the time. You can look for answers and find them. You can show your gratitude, talk about your fears, and ask for help.

Types of Prayer

Pour out your grief when your heart is filled with sadness and despair. You may be at a loss for words. In prayer, you express to God what you are going through and talk to Him as you would a friend. You might say, "Dear Lord, I am at a loss for words. I just know my heart is cracked in a million pieces. You, the Almighty, know what I am going through. Please help me understand."

Ask for comfort as a way to reach out to God in your grief. Comfort is seeking freedom from your pain. You could pray, "Dear Heavenly Father, relieve me of the feelings of guilt and grief over the loss of my loved one."

Ask for healing so that God brings His almighty powers to you. It is said, "Ask and you shall receive." Ask with prayer, and God will heal. "God, I ask you to heal my shattered heart that I will have the courage and the strength to carry on."

Ask for peace against the confusion in your heart. "Dear Lord, you are the Almighty. I need the inner peace that you alone can bring. Calm my anxious spirit. The if-only's and what-if's fill my heart with needless worry. Please take them away."

Prayer for hope is the desire to have things change and get better. "God, this is me, your servant and disciple. I am in a horrible place, and I now plead you to give me hope for a better future that I may see daylight again, and I may find joy."

God uses sorrow as His way of making us strong. We may not see what the purpose is, but God will reveal it. "Dear Heavenly Father, I am sorrowful, down on my knees and desperate. I do not understand why this is happening. I know that you use the sorrowful to help others. I am having a tough time. Please reveal to me how you will use me and my grief for the good."

God is using me to help others in their loss journey. Without a doubt, I know that God has given me all the tools, resources, and beliefs to survive this season. God does not choose the strong to lead but gives the weak, sorrowful, and tired the strength to lead. I am one of those weak, sorrowful, and tired ones.

Be open to God as your higher power. If He is not your higher power, then seek a higher power. Surrendering control is not easy to do. It is one of the best things I have ever done. I must do it every day. It is easy to rise and start my day with my agenda. What are my plans? What are my goals? What am I going to accomplish? Then I realize it is not about what I want to do. It is about God's will. I must stop and ask God His wish for me. What does He want me to do? Surrendering is a process. Give control back to God. I am not in control. Ask God to help and openly give the control to Him. Life goes so much better when I surrender.

No matter what I do, I must be a servant of God. I am His messenger, His disciple, the example of a loving Christian woman. The Three Phases to Move through Grief to Healing process is my ministry, and my opportunity to do good on God's behalf. I ask God to tell me who He wants me to touch and impact for His glory.

Learn About God

If you are questioning if there is a God, visit several churches and find one you are comfortable with. Many churches offer classes to those who are checking out the possibility that God exists. In many churches, they offer a class to ask and discuss life's big questions. Participating in the Alpha Course offers a chance to ask such questions and explore the Christian faith. Take the class and make the decision yourself. You may want to ask a friend to join you for moral support. Talking to God and expressing your deepest thoughts can be emotional.

In your darkest hour, you may feel buried and unable to cope. Think of yourself as a seed that has been planted in the soil. Seeds need to be in the dark for a season to sprout and grow. Look for what God is preparing you for. What plans does He have for you?

Forgiveness

My daughter Courtney died in an unlicensed daycare accident. At the time, her dad was traveling for his job, and I was working long and unusual hours, either 6:00 a.m. to 3:00 p.m. or 2:00 p.m. to sometimes 2:00 a.m. Traditional daycare was not an option. The woman, Faith, to whom I entrusted Courtney, was referred by a neighbor and was a grandmother. I knew that she loved and cared for Courtney.

Faith's childcare operation and facility were not licensed; thus, it was not under the scrutiny of authorities for safety. Courtney was put down for a nap and, due to negligence, she never woke up. It was the babysitter's fault that my daughter died. There was no question about it.

Unbeknownst to me, Faith had been warned by the authorities to either become licensed or stop providing daycare. I attended Faith's arraignment. The District Attorney asked if Courtney's dad and I wanted to press charges. We agreed that she was suffering just like we were. That was her sentence, and she would have to live with it.

However, due to this negligent accident and a prior violation, the District Attorney pressed criminal charges. Faith, a grandmother, served ninety days in jail for involuntary manslaughter resulting in death.

How was it that the DA pressed charges and I did not pursue civil suit? Even from the very beginning, I knew it was up to me to forgive Faith for a terrible mistake, error in judgment and, ultimately, the death of my daughter. I just knew then that if I did not forgive her, it would eat me alive. Over time, the anger, resentment, and unforgiveness would do more harm to me than it would ever do to her.

In 1991, I was not an active Christian. Forgiveness was simply the right thing to do. I was able to express my compassion for what Faith was going through.

Forgiveness is getting rid of negative thoughts, feelings, and behaviors directed at an offender and developing positive thoughts, feelings, and behaviors directed at this same person.

When Connor died, I also felt the need to forgive. I could have hated him, been angry, and become furious. He left me. He hurt me. Why did he not talk to me? Remember, as we have gone through this process, that poor mental health is directly related to the negative stories we tell ourselves. I could continue to blame Connor for all the things he did. I decided that was not a good choice. I did not want to be angry at my son, overriding any possibility of having good memories with and about him.

The anger could have kept me from sleeping, moving through my grief, and healing. This time, I knew it was biblical to forgive. A quick Google search about forgiveness results in a number of Bible verses about it. I want to be like Christ and forgive Connor. This has made my loss journey manageable and allowed me to move forward.

Whether you believe in the biblical principle of forgiveness or simply doing the right thing, think about who you need to forgive. That person might even be you. In the pursuit of self-forgiveness, you will return to feeling like living sooner than later with less suffering along the way.

These are options and suggestions for you. I know what my faith has done for me.

Mediums

A very dear friend gave me a gift certificate for one reading with a medium. Generally speaking, mediums purportedly mediate communication between us and spirits of the dead. I really struggled with accepting this gift. Even though it was from a Christian friend whom I believed would not lead me wrong, I had an inner sense that it was wrong, that it was not Godly, and quite possible was satanic.

I consulted Mary, who is a friend and pastor, about working with a medium. She unequivocally told me, "No, do not do it. It is demonic, and the Bible strongly tells us to have no part of it. I will not beat around the bush, Peggy. It is witchcraft and no matter what they tell you, you will open doors you wish you had never opened, and those spirits will torment you."

Mary continued, "Let Connor rest in peace. You do not need to do this, because God is good. You can depend on him. Peace my friend." In spite of her extremely strong warning, I still was not 100 percent positive whether working with a medium was as bad as she said.

This was just a few months after Connor died. My grief was deep, my pain terrible, and I was seeking relief from it. I was not in a healthy mental state. However, I felt if I talked to Connor, even if through a medium, I would feel better. My daughters would feel better too. I did not want to deny us any chance of healing.

I was not totally convinced. I needed more information, so I made an appointment with the medium, not for a reading though. Rather, I wanted to pepper her with questions regarding Christianity and mediums, giving her the opportunity to explain why she believed her work was actually from God.

Staci proceeded to tell me she connected with angels and not directly with the dead. She told me it was not against what the Bible says. She spoke confidently that if God did not want her to be able to communicate with those in heaven, He would not have given her the skills that allowed her to do this. In my grief, I believed her.

I decided to schedule a call. I felt it was all right to meet with her. I desperately wanted to know *why*. Why did Connor take his life? I was not willing to wait another thirty years or so until I died and met Connor in heaven to find out.

The reading was completed over the phone, and my daughters were included in the session. The medium explained that my son probably would not use words; he would use pictures, signs, and places to respond to her connection. The girls and I sat on the couch with the phone on the table with the speaker on, so we all could hear what she said.

Staci started by being silent and allowing Connor to connect with her. The first thing he showed her was a brown bag. The brown bag was the darkness that he could not escape. He could not get away from it. He could not remove it. Therefore, his solution was to end it all. I can tell you, I had no idea he was in so much pain. He had shared some of it with his older sister the week before his death, but she did not feel his challenges would lead him to take his life. He also shared that he was sorry. He was sorry for the pain he was causing us. If he had known the pain it would put us through, he would not have done it.

I could not blame Connor for our pain. He did not intentionally want to cause us heartache. He was in the moment and decided to end it all. He was not thinking clearly. He felt there was no hope of getting out of the darkness. He just had to put an end to his suffering. While I do not agree with his decision, I am grateful he is at peace. That I can accept.

I admit that the messages received through the medium were very comforting. I felt better knowing why Connor took his life. As mentioned earlier in this book, trying to understand *why* is the biggest obstacle in accepting death by suicide.

However, working with a medium has caused me a great deal of stress. The more I study God's word, the more I understand Mary's warning about mediums being the work of Satan.

I began to have an inner gnawing of something being spiritually wrong with me. I sought spiritual guidance from several people. All of them confirmed not to work with mediums by citing

Deuteronomy 18:11 (NCV), "Do not let anyone try to control others with magic, and do not let them be mediums or try to talk with the spirits of dead people."

This has been a dilemma for me on my spiritual journey. My pastor helped me understand that God was using this experience to draw me closer to Him and that instead of receiving comfort through mediums, I can turn to Him for comfort and peace.

While it may seem like a good idea to use a medium to connect with your child, you can also see the inner turmoil it has caused me. My suggestion is to explore your beliefs honestly and thoroughly before opening that door. Adding this to my grief has been horrible. I want to focus on healing, but this has tormented me.

Angelic Signs

The death of my son has taken me on a powerful spiritual journey and recognizing the presence of angels is no exception. An angel is a messenger who is sent to announce or proclaim, to give messages to humans. Angels are physical beings that dwell in heaven. It also means that a message sent from heaven is delivered by a physical being called an angel.

Angels surround us. From the first book of the Bible to the last book of Revelation, angels play an important role in scripture and are active throughout the story of God's people. Angels are powerful, fascinating, and known to appear in many different ways and diverse situations.

I am speaking of guardian angels who assist you in your time of need. They are appointed by God to help you. They are not your servant but are servants who are commissioned to protect God's people. Psalm 91:11, "For He will command his Angels concerning you to guard you in all your ways." Angels can also serve as ministers in moments of despair, Matthew 4:11, "Then the devil left him, and angels came and attended him."

Angels are to be found everywhere. They bring hope to God's people. You just need to remember to pray and ask for their intercession. Prayer gives angels permission to intercede on your behalf and offer aid.

Angels bring messages of peace and calm into your life, so you may live with purpose. God is not standing on the sidelines and wanting you to be in pain. He will send His angles to help you during your season of grief.

The Bible proclaims angels are around us and are guarding us. "See, I am sending an angel ahead of you to guard you along the way and to bring you to the place I have prepared," as recorded in Exodus 23:20. Although the Bible does not offer us details about angels appointed to us, we cannot disregard they are out there.

Angels are beautiful and majestic beings unlike anything we know. They make their presence known in a variety of ways.

My Experiences with Angels

I missed the first sign ever sent to me, because I was not looking for it. On the day of my son's funeral, I went for an early morning run. Running has always been an outlet for me and a way to ground myself. That morning the sunrise was spectacular. It was one of the most beautiful ones I have ever seen. For a December day, it was unusually warm, the wind was still, and the sky filled with cotton ball clouds. As the sun peeked over the horizon, deep shades of orange, yellow, and pink reflected off the clouds, intensifying their hue.

I had to stop my run and stand in awe of the beauty. I took a picture to add to my collection of sunrises. If you were to ask me to name two of my favorite things, I would answer sunrises and sunsets. You see, my son and I shared a love of them. On that day, my angel was sending me a message that I would be okay, that my son loved me, and more importantly that sunrises are my signs to remind me that he is with me. I did not understand his message then, but I do now.

Symbols

Your angel may send you simple signs. These signs are seen as symbols associated with love and happiness such as butterflies, rainbows, birds, or other positive images.

It is believed by some that feathers, sometimes white, and coins are left by angels as a reminder of the angelic presence in your life. Many people also believe coins placed in your path were left there by your deceased loved one or as gifts from your angel.

However, not all symbols have the same meaning to everyone. What determines whether you are receiving a sign from an angel is the significance of the object or the behavior of it. For example, perhaps a bluebird sits on your windowsill for ten minutes and carefully watches you as if it wants to take in every move you make. It does not fly away as you open the door and then hops onto the railing of your deck. This is unusual behavior for a bluebird, which would normally fly away in a matter of moments when it first sees you. This could be an angel visiting you.

Angelic energy is powerful, which can be directed toward you as well as an electrical devise around you. A light may flicker or turn itself on with no clear reason. You might experience seeing lights when your eyes are closed. Your inner vision can be filled with sparkling, glowing energy.

Orbs are another way angels let you know they are present. You may see them in your mind's eye or may even capture them in photographs. Other ways that you may feel and experience your angel is through cloud formations, gentle breezes, familiar scents, hearing familiar music, or hearing a message in your mind.

Raise Your Awareness

In order to feel an angel's presence, you need to slow down, which allows you to become more in tune with them. It opens the door for more signs in the natural world, so they can deliver more messages. Raising your awareness that these signs are not simply coincidences will help you understand you have miraculous and wonderful God-given angels supporting you. Regardless of your religious beliefs, signs such as rainbows, bluebirds, a particularly eye-catching sunrise, and lights turning on let you know you are not alone.

I believe that when you increase your perception of God's special messengers — angels — that you will see more signs. They are already there if you are now open to seeing them.

CHAPTER 18

CONCLUSION: YOU CAN EXPERIENCE HOPE AND HEALING

Hope and healing start with acceptance. Recently a friend whose child died by suicide asked me after Connor died, "When did you know you would be okay?" I must say her question made me pause and think. It is not a black-or-white answer.

After a few moments of reflection, I told her that, from the beginning, I promised I would allow myself to grieve. That meant if I did not feel like seeing anyone, I stayed home. I was okay with it. If I cried in the grocery store, it was what it was. There was no shame in being sad. If someone asked me why I was crying, I answered, "Because I miss my son."

Strangers, friends, and family were extremely compassionate in those moments of public display of grief and understood when

I did not want to be with anyone. The love I received helped me to understand I would be okay, that I would survive my loss, and there would be a day when I would be happy again.

In hindsight, it was my acceptance of what I was feeling in my loss journey that helped me to move through it. I accepted that it was okay to cry, to not want to be around others, and to have a hole in my heart. I understood these are all normal because, as humans, we mourn the loss of loved ones.

My grief journey is mine to walk. No one can do the work for me. I must be open to moving through the pain to heal. Likewise, your grief journey is yours to walk. No one can do the work for you. And you must be open to moving through the pain to heal.

However, I had others help me get through it. I did not do it alone. I leaned into my chaplain, friends, family and used other tools I developed — the tools I am presenting in this book.

Taking that first step — accepting where I was in my grief and that it was natural to cry and be sad — made it easier for me to move forward.

She then asked for any advice I could give her. I thought about it and told her: "Start by accepting that you have experienced loss. It is a horrible place to be. Once you have grasped that thought, it will be easier to process your loss and start moving through your grief. It worked for me."

Appreciation for Life

Other ways that I have seen a positive change is the way I appreciate life. Worrying about "stuff" is no longer important. The stuff is the latest smartphone, current-year car, fashion clothes, or the hottest watch. You know what your stuff is.

Life is too short. Live in the moment. Stop and smell the roses. These are all true statements and things we might consider even more now that our children are gone. Our hearts are so deeply wounded because of the moments we will never experience with our children.

What is crucial is our current relationships with friends and family. I know that I say "I love you" to family members even more than ever. I prefer having experiences together instead of giving material objects.

Serving others is a great way to expand beyond ourselves. One of my mentors' sums this up beautifully: "When you are having a bad day, take a moment to make someone else's day." Look for opportunities to help another person. Make a conscious decision to open a door, smile, say hello, let someone in line, forgive another driver's road rage, or buy someone else's coffee. These are just a few impromptu day-to-day things you can do.

In addition to small daily acts of service, I love to plan larger events and give back. I host an annual gratitude brunch. I wanted to bring my friends together and celebrate our friendships — new and old alike. From brunch, the event morphed into assembling winter care packages for the homeless. We collect donations for essential items and put them in bags to give to homeless people as we cross paths in our day-to-day activities.

I must say that was difficult the year after Connor passed away. Hosting an event like this takes planning, coordinating efforts, and time. I felt like I was in a fog and did not know what I was doing. By using the framework mentioned in this book, I pulled off a successful event.

What charitable organization is on your heart that you would like to give back to? It could be one that your child would appreciate you donating your time to in their memory. Your child is looking down on you and saying, "Way to go. Thanks for doing this." Helping others is so impactful and positive. It helps those whom you serve, while at the same time your body produces feel-good endorphins that elevate your mood and reduce depression and anxiety.

A Wedding Story

Last weekend I attended a wedding for a young couple. The bride and groom were absolutely stunning. We sat through a light rain in a beautiful fall setting with aspen trees boasting gorgeous gold, yellow, and orange leaves. The air was crisp, and anticipation was in the air.

The reception included a buffet, open bar, and photo booth. The usual toasts were given with high accolades for the bride and groom.

The party really started rocking when the dancing began. The dance floor became a mosh-pit of people of all ages celebrating the marriage of their friends and family members. I just loved watching the wave of bodies sway, jump, and bounce to some familiar and many not-so-familiar songs. It is unusual for me not to be in the middle of that mosh-pit, but a recent surgery kept me from doing so.

I sat quietly at the table and observed great excitement in all the partygoers' faces. Smiles were rampant and body language suggested nothing but happiness — happiness in the moment to welcome the bride and groom to the wonderful institution of marriage.

I cherished the vibrancy. My daughters were with me, which made this even more of a celebration. However, I could not help but to stop and think about my son. He and the bride knew each other. They grew up together. They were only three months apart in age. As I watched from my table, I could clearly picture Connor dancing, twirling, and smiling. He should have been there. He should have been celebrating with his childhood friend, his sisters, and myself.

The bride made her rounds to greet the guests, me included. She thanked me for coming and noted that she really appreciated it. She then asked if I saw Connor. At first, I thought she was talking about another boy named Connor. I told her no. She then proceeded to tell me there was a picture of my son, Connor, on the memorial table, along with other friends and relatives who passed away.

Wow! I was taken aback. This was not something I would have ever thought of. My son was included in their wedding event. All the accolades of praise to the bride and groom were affirmed in that simple gesture. I immediately rushed to the table to see his picture. Connor was smiling, happy, and giving two thumbs up.

I am still reeling from this gesture of love and kindness from the bride and groom. Connor's memory is not forgotten. His memory lives on. Thank you. Thank you. Thank you.

It is helpful to keep in mind that others will continue to love, remember, and honor your child. They will not be forgotten. Starting with acceptance — and then using the process and tools presented in this book — will allow you to move through your grief to healing.

Volunteering

If you could do something to help push back the darkness of grief, would you do it? One way to channel your once-positive energy that is now so dark is to redirect it toward something that is productive and meaningful. Volunteering is a great way to achieve new meaning and purpose in your life. Studies show that helping others dumps dopamine, a feel-good hormone, into your brain, resulting in increased happiness. Happiness affects your ability to process your grief.

Many groups desperately need volunteers. Without volunteers who share their time and talent, many of these organizations would cease to exist.

My coaching clients ask me when it is a good time to start volunteering. Many tell me they want to be further along in their healing before stepping out to help others. My response is that volunteering helps to get them to that place. You do not need to be perfect, recovered, and healed to help others. Volunteering is forward focused versus dwelling on the past. As a volunteer, you gain the opportunity to learn new skills, develop old ones, and have a positive impact on your community.

Volunteering can increase your output of dopamine, which is responsible for feelings of pleasure, satisfaction, and motivation. Volunteering can be a meaningful way to pay tribute to your loved one. It honors the physical connection you once had and respects them by helping others. Your loved one can be the inspiration and reason for paying it forward.

Volunteering also takes your mind off your own grief, even if for a short while. (Remember it is okay and natural to not think of your loved one all the time.) This gives you the chance to step back and see the bigger picture. Taking a reprieve from suffering allows you to be immersed in something that is fulfilling by focusing on others.

Volunteering comes in many forms. For example, you may choose to reach out to others who are grieving while sharing your coping skills. You have found you are moving through your own challenges, and it is a good time to offer guidance to others who are struggling. Your ability to empathize has risen dramatically, and you more fully understand their battles. Having a cause to put your time and effort into is a wonderful way to support others.

Although the idea of volunteering might seem crazy in this season of your life, before you totally disregard it, I encourage you to find something, somewhere to step out of your grief and help someone else. You will be in a fresh environment, meet new people, and even find yourself laughing again. You will begin to reconnect with the person you used to be and tap into that once-positive energy you used to have. I really do think you will feel that a load has been lifted from your shoulders.

Nikki's Story

During crisis, people either put their head in the sand or rise above it. I prefer to look for the positive. Through a recent conversation, I helped my friend Nikki move from seeing only the negative to seeing the positive. This was not an easy transition. She knew something was not right about her attitude. She had the feeling she was pushing friends away and did not know why. She came to me because she was feeling lonely.

Nikki's daughter passed away two years ago. We had a wonderful conversation about her daughter. She was so kind and loving. She had gotten that from Nikki but now, since her daughter was gone, Nikki was not like that anymore. She was negative, pushed friends and family away, and was not happy.

I told her I understood all of it. It is not easy to be positive when your child is gone. She agreed and with a barely audible voice asked, "How do I get back to who I was?" My heart went out to her, because I have seen the pain of being lost, not being the person you were before the loss of your child, and totally confused about what to do next.

We spent some time talking about who Nikki was before her daughter died. We looked at what had inspired her. She wrote a list of the things she wanted to do. She told me the values she lived for. She shared her "before" dreams.

Next, we discussed how she would live up to those values, be inspired, and how she would now fulfill those dreams. Nikki wrote five positive affirmations about herself that she read three times a day. She started paying attention to the words she heard from those she admired. She listened for the positive in what they said. She then implemented those thoughts into her conversations.

Within a week, she saw a shift in the way she spoke and felt about herself. She felt good about what she was saying and, ultimately, she was reconnecting with those she had alienated. Nikki found that small steps in personal growth were huge in her new-found appreciation for life.

Rely on Your Tribe

Last night as I was walking my dog, my thoughts turned to my son, which they frequently do when I walk. I found myself doubting how many years it has been since he died. I literally stopped in my tracks and counted on my fingers.

A combination of disbelief, denial, and the pace of life caused me to doubt my calculations. I miss my son and my daughter who passed many years earlier. I think of them often, yet I find myself living a joy-filled life. I pondered how I could be happy, laugh, and love with two children in heaven.

Walking in the dark with only a few streetlights and a cold crispness in the air, I had the quietness and the space to think clearly. I realized I have a good life, because I have learned a variety of tools and coping skills. Each of them played a role in my healing. Sometimes I used one tool or coping skill more than another.

My tribe includes those who supported me since my first loss in 1991 and those who helped me in 2018. The people in my tribe have changed over thirty years. They were friends, family, and strangers through love, caring, and similar life experiences who made a difference.

To describe your tribe, think of your circle of friends, family, and others as three circles. Just like a Venn diagram they start to overlap and come together in supporting you in your child loss journey. Your inner circle is a mixture of your closest friends, family, and others.

My tribe talked to me in person and on the phone. They sent text messages and emails with words of encouragement. When I needed a real hug, they wrapped their arms around me. Physical touch is part of healing. Their hugs were warm, genuine, and meaningful. When we spoke on the phone, their voices conveyed love, caring, and compassion.

If you are struggling with your grief, consider finding those who will support you in person and through live interaction. Science indicates that in-person activities help with healing. Remember, social media is a form of isolation. In isolation, you will not heal. As humans, we are meant to be with others, live with others, support each other, and be supported. Relying on my tribe — near and far — made a difference for me, and I am forever grateful for those in my inner circle who literally stood by my side in my grief.

Your Next Steps

Congratulations, you made it to the last chapter of *Survive Your Child's Suicide: How to Move through Grief to Healing*. This book was designed to give you coping skills, tools, and healthy options to move through your grief. I have used all the tools. You may not. You get to choose which ones you like and leave the ones that do not work for you. Remember, there is no right or wrong way to grieve, however, there are healthy ways to do so.

Journaling is a tool that even now I consistently utilize. It is useful no matter your circumstances. You can do it anywhere and anytime. The other tools are used as needed on my grief journey. I have learned them and practiced them. They help me when I struggle with accepting my circumstances by providing me permission to grieve and to heal. When fear presents itself, I can identify it, face it, and overcome it, because I understand it.

Your recovery will come full circle when you incorporate physical, mental, emotional, and spiritual health. Exercise, nutrition, mindset, affirmations, and belief in a higher power are components of your healing.

I now stand on the other side of the rope bridge. The vast abyss with its perils and obstacles is behind me. I am grateful that I am here today. You too can navigate the rope bridge. You can overcome the obstacles and stand on the other side — the side with healing, hope, and joy.

In the past thirty years, I learned how to deal with death, the loss of my parents, sister, and other relatives. I did not know then what those experiences were setting me up for, but I know now. I have a calling to help other mothers travel this journey. I bear witness to their loss like no other person can. I am their resource who will listen, care, and understand what they are going through.

Now, you know that I am a grief coach. Based on what I have experienced, I recommend you work with someone and get the support that you so desperately want and need. What is important is that you move forward.

Before you do, before you make a decision, there are three criteria I recommend you use to help you decide who you will work with:

- Does the person you want to work with have personal experience with child loss? This is an incredibly important criteria.
- Does this person have the passion to be working as a grief coach? I believe loss travelers deserve to have support and guidance from someone who has walked this journey. As a result they are passionate about helping others learn to live with their grief and find joy.
- Have they personally used the tools and techniques they offer to you? The tools I share with you are 100 percent responsible for me being here and able to offer you support.

Why You Are Here

You are here because your child died by suicide. I am sorry that you are going through this. You are reading this book, because you want help. You want help to make it through a difficult season in your life. This book and the process I present are the support you have been looking for. My purpose is to help you navigate your loss journey and to support you in your desire to heal.

It is my dream that you found this process helpful as a fellow loss traveler. We are on this journey together. If you found this book to be impactful, please do not keep it to yourself. Please, please share it with a friend or family member who would benefit from learning these tools.

Grief is a continuous journey. It is a long and winding road. There will be ups and downs. Some days will be better than others. It gets better. I know. I understand. I've walked in your shoes. However, it does not get better by itself. You will need to use the tools that I've given you. In the beginning, it may feel awkward or feel like they are not working. Keep practicing. This is about progress and not perfection.

The tools will help. Use them often and where needed. They will come in handy when difficult situations occur. They will help you when you anticipate grief sneaking up on you. They will help you feel like you can handle any situation that arises. Because you can.

APPENDIX 1

SUICIDE RISK
FACTORS AND
WARNING SIGNS

The following risk factors and warning signs are a combination of information from the Suicide Prevention Resource Center, American Foundation for Suicide Prevention, and U.S. Centers for Disease Control and Prevention.

Know the Risk Factors

Risk factors are attributes that increase the likelihood that someone will consider, attempt, or die by suicide. This list is not all inclusive and cannot predict a suicide attempt, but it will create awareness. Risk factors include:

- Mental health disorders, specifically mood disorders, schizophrenia, anxiety disorders, and certain personality disorders (Research has found that about 90 percent of individuals who die by suicide experience mental health illness. Experiencing a mental illness is the number-one risk factor for suicide.)
- Experience of knowing others who have died by suicide (in real life or via the media and Internet)
- Alcohol and other substance abuse
- Hopelessness
- Belief that suicide is a noble resolution and benefits others
- Impulsive and/or aggressive tendencies
- Shortage of healthcare, notably mental health, and substance abuse treatment
- History of trauma or abuse
- Stigma associated with seeking help
- Major physical illnesses
- Limited social support and sense of isolation
- Previous suicide attempts
- Familial history of suicide
- Local cluster of suicide
- Job or financial loss
- Easy access to lethal means
- Loss of relationships

Know the Warning Signs

If you or someone you know has been or is newly exhibiting these behaviors, seek help immediately. In the United States the

National Suicide Prevention Lifeline is 800-273-8255. You will receive 24/7 support. The following behaviors may increase after a painful event, loss, or change in your/their life. Watch for these warning signs:

- Showing rage or talking about seeking revenge
- Talking about others who died by suicide
- Talking about wanting to die or to kill themselves
- Making plans to have children, spouse, or pets to be taken care of
- Talking about feeling hopeless or having no reason to live
- Increasing the use of alcohol or drugs
- Acting anxious or agitated
- Taking increased interest with life-threatening sports
- Sleeping too little or too much
- Withdrawing or isolating themselves
- Talking about being a burden to others
- Talking about feeling trapped or being in unbearable pain
- Looking for a way to kill themselves such as searching online or buying a gun
- Extreme mood swings
- Changing spending patterns

COMMON QUESTIONS WITH ANSWERS ABOUT GRIEF

Q: "Is it normal to grieve?"

A: Absolutely. It is completely normal to grieve. Grief is so normal that it is expected to be a part of your life forever after the event. Its intensities will go up and down based on time of year and how long it's been since the event, but the grief will likely always be there in one form or another, existing alongside other emotions and feelings like joy, happiness, and more.

Q: "Are mourning and grief the same?"

A: No, mourning and grief are not the same. Grief is the emotion you feel, the state of mind you are in, when you experience the loss of a relationship through death, divorce, and so forth. Mourning is the traditional or inventive activation of grief; the movements you go through as you experience grief. Mourning is best defined as acts or outward expressions of grief. Some common examples of mourning can include preparing for a funeral, wearing black, or sharing memories or stories about your loved one.

Q: "Is it okay to be angry when I grieve?"

A: Yes, it is absolutely okay to be angry when you grieve. The goal is to not hurt yourself or others during the times you experience anger. Anger is normal when grieving as you come to terms with what happened to the person you love. You may feel that the situation is unfair. Maybe you are angry at someone who caused something to happen. Maybe you are angry at the person who died. Maybe you are angry with yourself. Anger is a way to sort through the emotions and help your brain come to terms with the events. Prolonged anger, however, can be an issue as can anger that causes you to hurt yourself or others.

Q: "What types of people have the hardest time when losing someone?"

A: There is no possible way to answer this question. Everyone deals with grief and loss differently, and it is important not to compare your loss to another person's loss.

Q: "How long will this last?"

A: I wish there were a standard answer. It is individual and your response to it depends on how long your grief will last. You are on a grief journey and, as you use the tools presented in this book, the path will become less bumpy and the return to life without your loved one will become easier.

Q: "Someone told me their loss was more difficult than mine. Is that true? Can grief be ranked?"

A: Grief cannot be ranked. Someone else's loss is not the same as yours. The relationship you have with the person who died is what matters most in terms of the intensity of grief. No one's grief is more or less than another's.

Q: "What is bereavement?"

A: Bereavement is the period of grief and mourning after a death.

Q: "Is it okay to try to push your feelings away when grieving?"

A: To an extent, yes, it is okay to push your feelings away when grieving, but you will need to deal with them at some point. This is a form of avoidance.

Q: "Is crying a good way to grieve?"

A: Yes, absolutely, crying is a good way to grieve. Crying releases endorphins and makes you feel better.

Q: "Will your grief be gone after a good cry?"

A: No. But will you feel better giving yourself this time to really feel the emotion and let it pass through you.

Q: "Should I talk to people about my feelings?"

A: Yes, you should absolutely talk to people about your feelings. Talk to friends. Talk to family. Talk to a grief support group. Talk to your cat. Heck, talk to yourself! And remind friends and family (and maybe even yourself) that what you need right now is for someone to listen, not to placate you.

Q: "Is it okay to want to be alone when grieving?"

A: Yes, it is okay to want to be alone when grieving. Sometimes when you are grieving, you might separate yourself from people for a little bit. And that is okay. You are processing your feelings. That said, folks who are grieving have also said in studies that the number-one thing that is most helpful during grieving is being around friends and family. Being around friends and family at this time may seem difficult or impossible, but it is a healthy thing — and one that can make you feel a lot better, too.

Q: "Is there a right way to grieve?"

A: No, there is no single right way to grieve. However, there is a healthy way to grieve. You are reading this book and learning how to grieve in a wholesome way.

Q: "My doctor or therapist wants me to take medication, and I do not want to. What should I tell them?"

A: Ask them what they see in you that warrants the need for medication. Tell them why you are reluctant to take medication and ask if they think that you will not get better without it. There may be a time for medication, but do not take it blindly. I suggest you try additional alternative methods along with medication. You may want to re-read the chapter addressing physical health.

Q: "My best friend, who was there for me before my beloved died, no longer talks to me and avoids me. Why cannot my friend support me?"

A: Death changes you. You are no longer the person you were before your loss. Your friend may not be able to relate to you now. This is unfortunate because it is another loss for you. You can have a heart-to-heart conversation and ask your friend if there is something you did to create this distance. You can also tell your friend that you need his or her extra support. But remember that some people are not comfortable with the topic of grief. They do not know what to say or are afraid of saying the wrong thing, so they avoid anything associated with loss — and your very presence is a reminder of loss. Your circle of friends and support will change. It is okay if they cannot be there for you right now. Remove that expectation, and your friendship can stay intact.

Q: "I do not think I'll ever get over the death of my child. What do you suggest I do?"

A: The death of a loved one is not something to "overcome." I gently suggest that you look at the way you see this tragedy. Death is like an amputation, and you do not just grow a new limb. Learning how to live with this significant loss in a healthy way should become your focus instead of simply trying to move past your loss. Using the tools presented in this book, you will learn how to think differently about your loss and be able to move through your grief to healing.

APPENDIX 3

ADDITIONAL GRIEF AFFIRMATIONS

A s you read in Chapter 16, using affirmations is a simple and easy way to modify your thinking patterns. Grief affirmations can be said anytime and anywhere. You might be surprised how well a grief affirmation can lift your spirits.

Remember, you do not need to memorize your favorite affirmations. You can write them on index cards and carry them with you. I find that having two sets of ten affirmations is convenient — one set for home and the other set in my purse.

In addition to the list presented in Chapter 16, you can choose from the following grief affirmations:

- In my sadness, I love myself.
- It's okay to take time to grieve.
- I let go of my sorrow but hold on to my love for my loved one.

- I am willing to release any negative fearful idea from my mind and body and life.
- It's okay to be angry at having to grieve.
- I feel my grief but do not wallow in it.
- I relax and let all the feelings flow through today.
- I have lived and loved. I give and receive love today.
- Grieving takes time. I am patient with my healing process.
- I forgive anyone close to me who has died.
- I feel my angels holding me today as I grieve.
- I accept what I cannot change and find the courage to change the things I can.
- My life has purpose, and I live today in compassion and love.
- I look for the rainbows after the storm.
- I will rest today when I need it.
- I'm through grieving today, and I move onto other emotions.
- I take care of myself as I heal.
- I am thankful for the time I shared with my loved one.

ABOUT THE BACK COVER

I t bears mentioning the significance of the back-cover pictures: Daniels Park, tie-dye, and the locket.

Connor, his older sister Brittany, and their friends frequently visited Daniels Park. It is located in Douglas County, Colorado, and is well known among the locals for the bison herd that roams the park and the spectacular mountain views spanning from Pikes Peak to Longs Peak. The park also offers wonderful cityscapes of downtown Denver and the Denver Tech Center. Even more breathtaking are the sunsets while facing the Rocky Mountains with the plethora of colors, shades, and hues.

To experience a sunset at Daniels Park with close friends and family is profound. The mountains and the rock formations provide the setting to have authentic and meaningful conversations. There is a deep and unexplainable peace to be had. No matter your religious preference, it is a place to connect with your higher power and experience the most extraordinary level of spirituality possible.

That is why Connor loved Daniels Park. That is why it was so important to have the back-cover picture taken there.

Connor's sisters — Brittany and Hannah — are in the picture with me. I am not the only one grieving for him. They too have been impacted by his premature departure. It is important to recognize their part in my grief healing. Without them, I would not be here.

Notice that all three of us are wearing tie-dye shirts. Connor loved tie-dye t-shirts. As a matter of fact, he would wear them under his dress shirts at work, especially on Fridays, which were deemed Tie-Dye Friday.

The locket was a gift I received after Connor died. It was hand-made by one of Brittany's coworkers and customized with charms specific to me — the colors of the stones, the angel wings, and the words "family" and "love."

When I hike, I take some of Connor's ashes with me, so I can spread them. To remember the places Connor has gone with me, I take a picture of the locket either dangling from a tree, strung over a log, or lying on a rock. Some of the places are where Connor and I hiked together before he passed. Others are new to him. I feel in my heart that Connor would enjoy the places he now gets to visit with me.

As I close the season in which I wrote this book, those places and things that used to cause pain and suffering are now precious memories to treasure. Daniels Park is no longer difficult to visit. Instead, I experience the same level of spirituality that Connor enjoyed. As for the locket, it brings me great joy to share new adventures with my son in a unique and special way.

ABOUT THE AUTHOR

S uicide death of a child rocks a parent's world to its inner core. Questions haunt you: Why did they do it? Why didn't they come to me? Why didn't I see it coming? How can I go on with my life when my child is gone?

In front of you is a vast abyss. One side is your present situation of pain and suffering. The other, hope and joy. What lies between is a rope bridge that can take you from grief to hope and healing. However, you must take the first step and trust that no matter how perilous it seems, you will survive.

Peggy Green has crossed that bridge not just once but twice. Her first child died in 1991, and then in 2018 her son died by suicide. The magnitude of her loss is immense. From her personal trials, she now helps other grieving mothers as a grief coach, speaker, and author.

As a grief coach, she combines fifteen years of fitness and nutrition coaching with her life experiences to develop a step-by-step process to move through grief. Her program — Three Phases to Move through Grief to Healing — is founded on restoring physical, mental, emotional, and spiritual health. In fact, Peggy's mission is to help women move through physical, mental, emotional, and

SURVIVE YOUR CHILD'S SUICIDE

spiritual suffering caused by child suicide, so they can live fulfilling and purposeful lives.

Peggy's first book, *Life After Child Loss: The Mother's Survival Guide to Cope and Find Joy*, is an Amazon bestseller. As a speaker and podcast guest, her message has been heard in nearly 100 countries. Her weekly *Thursday Thoughts* blog and email newsletter is inspirational and encouraging to thousands mourning the death of a loved one.

In her second book, *Survive Your Child's Suicide: How to Move through Grief to Healing*, she may be the first to teach acceptance as the first step in grief recovery.

Peggy volunteers for the American Foundation for Suicide Prevention and leads a community Pay It Forward group. She lives in Highlands Ranch, Colorado, near her two grown daughters and grandchildren. She finds joy in hiking, baking, spending time with her family, and appreciating sunrises and sunsets.

Peggy is available for grief coaching, addressing groups, and speaking at conferences. For more information on her books, workshops, and coaching program, please contact her via her website, www.theegriefspecialist.com.